P9-EAO-146

Jacob Lawrence: The *Frederick Douglass* and *Harriet Tubman* Series of 1938–40

Jacob Lawrence:
The *Frederick Douglass* and *Harriet Tubman* Series of 1938–40

Ellen Harkins Wheat

Hampton University Museum · Hampton, Virginia

in association with
UNIVERSITY OF WASHINGTON PRESS
Seattle and London

Copyright © 1991 Hampton University Museum and Ellen Harkins Wheat
Text © Ellen Harkins Wheat
Paintings and captions © Hampton University Museum
ALL RIGHTS RESERVED
No part of this book may be reproduced or transmitted in any form or by any means, electronic or mechanical, including photocopying, recording, or by any information storage and retrieval system, without permission in writing from Hampton University Museum, except in the case of brief quotations embodied in critical articles and reviews.

Library of Congress Cataloging-in-Publication Data appear at the end of the book.

ISBN 0–9616982–4–1 (softbound)
ISBN 0–9616982–5–x (cloth)

Set in type and printed by Meriden-Stinehour Press
Design by Christopher Kuntze

Editor, Lorna Price
Photographs of Jacob Lawrence's paintings by Scott Wolff

Softbound and cloth editions published by Hampton University Museum, Hampton University, Hampton, Virginia 23668

Distributed by University of Washington Press
P.O. Box 50096, Seattle, WA 98145–5096

PRINTED IN THE UNITED STATES OF AMERICA

The excerpt from the Frederick Douglass letter included as the epigraph for this book is reproduced with permission from the Schomburg Center for Research in Black Culture, New York Public Library.

COVER
FRONT: *Harriet Tubman* series, No. 7, 1939–40, by Jacob Lawrence.
BACK: (left) *Frederick Douglass* series, No. 13, 1938–39;
(right) *Harriet Tubman* series, No. 4, 1939–40.
Photographs by Scott Wolff.

FRONTISPIECE
Jacob Lawrence at work, 1990. Photograph by Chris Eden.

Man is the only picture making and picture appreciating animal in the world. . . . An element so distinctive and universal as this—manifesting itself in the earliest morning of intellectual life (for childhood delights in pictures) and rising among the rudest notions with the first dawnings of . . . civilization, lifting the thoughts and sentiments of men higher by every one of its triumphs—can hardly be too diligently cultivated, or its beneficial influence too highly estimated.

Frederick Douglass, in a letter to R. Koehler, Esq.
Rochester, New York
July 25, 1868

Contents

Foreword

HAMPTON UNIVERSITY is pleased to present Jacob Lawrence's *Frederick Douglass* and *Harriet Tubman* series in this extraordinary publication and exhibit. These powerful paintings, created over fifty years ago by one of America's greatest artists, continue to speak eloquently of human struggle, determination, and dedication. Lawrence depicted the lives of Frederick Douglass and Harriet Tubman in compelling and accessible works of art. His goal was to document the accomplishments of these two American heroes so that their contributions would not be forgotten. The paintings came to Hampton in 1967. Since that time they have provided inspiration and insight for Hampton students and for the community.

The enduring importance of America's historically black colleges and universities is perhaps most directly revealed through their critical role in nurturing, preserving, documenting, and transmitting African-American culture. Hampton University has been a leader in this area, establishing a collection of African art in the 1870s, beginning the collection of African-American music in the same decade, and becoming the first institution to collect African-American art in 1894 with the acquisition of Henry O. Tanner's renowned painting *The Banjo Lesson*. For much of the twentieth century, when most non-black museums and educational institutions did not value and did not collect African-American art or artifacts, Hampton has been one of the main repositories of African-American culture.

As we approach the twenty-first century, it is our desire to seek ways to disseminate to a broad audience the concepts, the values, and the visions embodied in Hampton's rich collections. That is the goal of this publication and exhibit. For that reason, we have endeavored to create a book appealing to a wide variety of interests: the text will inform art historians and historians, as well as non-specialists; the generous illustrations will satisfy the collector and connoisseur, and will serve appropriately as a story book for children. In keeping with Jacob Lawrence's original intent, we offer this book and the exhibition so that the work of Frederick Douglass, Harriet Tubman and other African-American heroes will remain in the American consciousness. We also offer the book and the exhibit so that recognition and appreciation of Jacob Lawrence and of other African-American artists will be advanced.

William R. Harvey
President
Hampton University

Preface

In 1967, Jacob Lawrence's *Frederick Douglass* and *Harriet Tubman* series joined the Hampton Institute College Museum collection, now the Hampton University Museum. The sixty-three paintings were part of a gift from the Harmon Foundation of hundreds of significant works of art by noted African-American artists.

A private foundation based in New York City, the Harmon Foundation began a pathbreaking program of support for African-American art in 1926. For four decades, the Foundation promoted individual artists, organized exhibitions, and supported art education. Hampton Institute was one beneficiary of these activities. In the late 1930s and early 1940s, the Foundation brought exhibitions to the Hampton campus. This relationship expanded through the years, resulting in the 1967 gift. The purpose, as expressed in a 1962 letter from the Foundation to the College, was to strengthen Hampton's art program,

. . . we also have this larger view, I believe, that eventually could put Hampton into a strategic position from the point of view of intercultural, interracial and international understanding through art.

Founded in 1868 for African-American education, Hampton University today is a private, small comprehensive university. Its Museum was also founded in 1868 to support the academic program and to enhance self-esteem, pride, and cross-cultural understanding. The Hampton University Museum is the oldest museum associated with any of America's historically black institutions. The collections, which include African, American Indian, Asian, Pacific, and African-American art, are world renowned.

In the past decade, recognition of Hampton's collection has grown with over 1000 works of art lent for exhibition to America's museums. "Jacob Lawrence: The Frederick Douglass and Harriet Tubman Series of Narrative Paintings," however, is the first national exhibition organized by the Hampton University Museum. This book is among our first major publications. Ap-preciation is due to the many organizations and individuals who made this project possible. First and foremost, gratitude is expressed to Jacob Lawrence for his confidence and support.

Ellen Harkins Wheat's participation was critical. The Museum is pleased to have collaborated with this careful and thoughtful scholar. We are equally pleased to have had the opportunity to work with Christopher Kuntze of Meriden-Stinehour Press, and are delighted that the University of Washington Press with Don Elle-good is assisting with the distribution.

Hampton received major funding from the Ford Foundation which made this publication possible. Appreciation is due to Ruth Mayleas and Peter Stanley for their encouragement. The John Sloan Memorial Foundation assisted with support for the exhibition. Gratitude is expressed to Mrs. Helen Farr Sloan who has been an important friend. The National Endowment for the Arts provided partial support for the preparation of the book manuscript. An Institute of Museum Services award to Hampton assisted with exhibition costs.

Hampton University Museum staff members Mary Lou Hultgren, Betty Belle, Heather Ampofo-Anti, Jeffrey Bruce, and Patrica Favor devoted many hours to this project. Reuben V. Burrell and Scott Wolff created excellent photographs of the works of art. Ron Cunningham undertook the conservation of the paintings. Liza Broudy and Jan Miller provided exhibit support.

Recognition is due to Dr. William R. Harvey, President of Hampton University. His support of art, of artists, and of the Hampton Museum has begun a renaissance of artistic activity at the University. It has also provided the basis for the exceptional cultural resources in the Hampton University Museum to achieve their potential in serving a broad and diverse audience.

Jeanne Zeidler
Director
Hampton University Museum

Acknowledgments

I HAVE BEEN privileged to work with Jacob Lawrence since 1979, first on my monograph *Jacob Lawrence, American Painter*. For the current book, both Lawrence and his wife, Gwendolyn Knight Lawrence, have participated in the research and have read the manuscript for accuracy, and I am indebted to them for their generous involvement.

Of the many people who contributed to this book and exhibition project, I am enormously grateful to Jeanne Zeidler, Director of the Hampton University Museum, for her interest and support. Without Jeanne's tenacity, this project could not have been realized. I am also grateful to Mary Lou Ulbrick Hultgren, Curator of the museum, and to the rest of the staff of the museum, for their work on the exhibition. I am thankful for funding from the National Endowment for the Arts for the research and writing of the manuscript, and for funding from the Ford Foundation for the publication of the book.

I am grateful to Peter Selz, Professor Emeritus, History of Art, University of California at Berkeley, for reading the manuscript and offering observations.

Several historians graciously consented to read the manuscript, and I am most appreciative of their thoughtful comments: John Hope Franklin, James B. Duke Professor Emeritus, Duke University; Thomas J. Pressly, Professor Emeritus of History, University of Washington; Nell Irvin Painter, Professor of History, Princeton University; the late Nathan Irvin Huggins, Director, W.E.B. DuBois Institute for Afro-American Research, Harvard University; John R. McKivigan, Managing Editor, Frederick Douglass Papers Project, Yale University; and C. Peter Ripley, Editor, Black Abolitionist Papers Project, Department of History, The Florida State University. I am responsible, however, for facts and interpretations in the book.

Many people were particularly helpful in my research and effort to find photographs: Sydney Kaplan, Professor of English, The University of Massachusetts; Carolyn Davis, Manuscript Librarian, The George Arents Research Library, Syracuse University; Julia Hotton, Director, and the staff at the Schomburg Center for Research in Black Culture, New York; and Patricia Willis, Curator, and Stephen Jones at the Beinecke Rare Book and Manuscript Library, Yale University.

Others generously contributed to the planning and development of the book and exhibition project: Jill Rullkoetter, Head of Education, Seattle Art Museum; Barbara Henry, Head of Education, Oakland Museum; Constance Rice, President of CWR, Inc., Seattle; Pamela McClusky, Associate Curator of The Art of Africa and Oceania, Seattle Art Museum; James Oliver Horton, Professor of History, George Washington University; Barbara A. Hail, Associate Director and Curator, Haffenreffer Museum of Anthropology, Brown University; and Kate Duncan, Assistant Professor of Art History, Arizona State University.

I want to recognize the work of Roland Cunningham, Jr., Senior Paintings Conservator, Smithsonian Institution, who carefully restored the paintings so that they would be at their best for the photographs and the exhibition.

Special thanks go to Don Ellegood, Director of the University of Washington Press, and to the staff of the Press, for their interest in the project and for undertaking the distribution of the book.

I also want to thank Gene Vike, Chair, Art Department, Western Washington University, for his support during my tenure as Visiting Assistant Professor of Art History there while I was finishing the manuscript.

I am grateful to Lorna Price, an extraordinary editor. Thanks also go to Shellie Tucker, the book's proofreader and indexer. The current photographs of Jacob Lawrence are the work of Chris Eden, a fine Seattle photographer, and I express my appreciation to him.

E.H.W.

Introduction

I WROTE this book to fulfill a personal commitment, that of documenting Jacob Lawrence's two most closely linked series, *Frederick Douglass* and *Harriet Tubman*. The paintings in these two sequences have been reproduced in various sources but never all together, nor have they been exhibited alone together in their entirety since their creation, except at the Hampton University Museum, their home.[1]

The heart of the book's concept has been, from the outset, to reproduce all the paintings in these two important series in full-page color with their narrative captions, as well as to fully document the paintings and captions for the first time. It was also my goal to make the book a permanent, comprehensive catalogue for the two series, and it was to Jeanne Zeidler, Hampton University Museum director, that I proposed the book and the exhibition project—a goal that her enthusiasm and energies have helped bring to fruition. Because these two series were painted sequentially and complement each other in subject and style, they are best appreciated when viewed together. Our reward is seeing these two great series of Jacob Lawrence's exhibited together with the attention they richly merit.

Fortunately, both series are owned by the Hampton University Museum and have been maintained in good condition. This is a notable advantage for posterity as well as for the researcher, because many of Lawrence's thematic sequences have been split up and dispersed over the course of half a century, and the obstacles to reassembling them for publication and exhibition are formidable; some pieces are even lost. The Hampton University Museum has owned the *Frederick Douglass* and *Harriet Tubman* series since 1967, when they were given to the University by the Harmon Foundation, a philanthropic organization that had been active in the period of the Harlem Renaissance and afterward, and had been interested in encouraging the artistic development of African-Americans.[2]

There can be no true comprehension of America's development as a nation without an understanding and appreciation of such great nineteenth century humanitarians as Frederick Douglass and Harriet Tubman, whose accomplishments have long been neglected in American historiography, or else altogether omitted. Some revisionists are working on correcting these oversights, but progress is slow. This book is therefore offered as more than a book about the art and the artist or a catalogue of the exhibition. It also explores the insufficiently documented contributions Douglass and Tubman made to the resolution of issues encompassed by the American Civil War. The effect of their efforts toward the ultimate abolition of slavery cannot be overestimated.

Frederick Douglass wrote four autobiographies;[3] the first one, of 1845 (*Narrative of the Life of Frederick Douglass, An American Slave, Written by Himself*), remains a dramatic testament of the man's struggle to achieve not only freedom from slavery but liberation of the life of the mind. Harriet Tubman was illiterate; Sarah Bradford's 1886 account of Tubman's accomplishments (*Harriet Tubman: The Moses of Her People*) is also very moving. Inexplicably, to my knowledge neither of these books is assigned reading in schools below college level, despite the importance of their subjects. I frequently receive inquiries from people who want to know more about Douglass and Tubman, as well as about Jacob Lawrence's series on them.

This book is offered, therefore, to help fill a need for the general reader, the teacher, and the student, as well as for the history of art. It is unique in treating just Douglass and Tubman together as great heroes of the same epoch. And because many of the facts surrounding their lives are relatively obscure to many readers of this book and viewers of Lawrence's paintings, I have provided lengthy notes to the text and the paintings, explaining historical events, issues, and persons referred to in the paintings' captions. Through this gesture, I hope to make this book especially useful to educators and other curious readers.

A significant part of this project has been the correction of the numbers of the *Douglass* series panels. Confusion existed because the series ended with a panel numbered "33" but there were only thirty-two paintings in the sequence; one in the middle was numbered "14–15" and had a double caption. I have sleuthed to decipher this mystery, to no avail. The artist cannot recall how this happened, but because he wishes to correct the problem once and for all, with his approval I have now numbered the *Douglass* series consecutively, panels 1 through 32, with panel 14 retaining the dual caption. (A more detailed discussion of this resolution is given in note 20 to Chapter 2, "The *Frederick Douglass* Series.")

When Jacob Lawrence parted company with the paintings of the two series around 1940, he recalls having given the Harmon Foundation a handwritten list of captions to accompany them. Typed caption labels are pasted to the backs of the works. Lawrence believes the Harmon Foundation typed the caption labels and affixed them to the panels. But the captions for both the series have come down in the literature over time with numerous errors. For this project, I have researched the material in the captions and then worked with Lawrence to correct typographical and factual errors in them. The paintings' captions are presented here essentially as the artist originally composed them but in their final, corrected, and authorized versions, in compliance with the textual sources to which they relate and in accordance with the artist's wishes.

The *Frederick Douglass* and *Harriet Tubman* series remain dear to Jacob Lawrence. The works came out of a period when he felt himself to be a participant in a worldwide artistic movement to improve the human condition. The subjects and issues of these two series still have great meaning to Lawrence, as he continues to reflect on the human struggle in his work. Through his interest in Frederick Douglass and Harriet Tubman and his eloquent painterly conceptions of their lives, Lawrence has given Americans much. He, too, is a great American humanitarian. To Jacob Lawrence and his wife and life's partner, Gwendolyn Knight Lawrence, this book and exhibition are dedicated.

Ellen Harkins Wheat
July 30, 1990

I've always been interested in history, but they never taught Negro history in the public schools. . . . I don't see how a history of the United States can be written honestly without including the Negro. I didn't do it just as a historical thing, but because I believe these things tie up with the Negro today. We don't have a physical slavery, but an economic slavery. If these people, who were so much worse off than the people today, could conquer their slavery, we certainly can do the same thing. They had to liberate themselves without any education. Today we can't go about it in the same way. Any leadership would have to be the type of Frederick Douglass. . . . How will it come about? I don't know. I'm not a politician. I'm an artist, just trying to do my part to bring this thing about. I had several reasons for doing this work, and these are some of them. . . . Another reason is that I have great admiration for the [lives of such people]. It's the same thing Douglass meant when he said, "Judge me not by the heights to which I have risen but by the depths from which I have come." There's so much to do, there's never any trouble to find subjects.

Jacob Lawrence, 1940

1
Jacob Lawrence and the Series Format

JACOB LAWRENCE painted the *Frederick Douglass* and *Harriet Tubman* series in the late 1930s during his early maturity. The two historical sequences present the dramatic biographies of these two American abolitionists who lived around the time of the Civil War. Taken together, the paintings have an extraordinary conceptual unity and visual eloquence, and although completed very early in Lawrence's career, these two series embody some of the artist's strongest work.

Jacob Lawrence grew up in Harlem during the Depression, and his career owes much to that heritage.[1] Lawrence received early training in the Harlem Art Workshops supported by the government under the Federal Art Project of the Works Progress Administration (WPA), and he attended the American Artists School in New York between 1937 and 1939 on scholarship; he was still a student when he began work on these two series of paintings. Lawrence served as an easel painter on "the Project" in Harlem at twenty-one and twenty-two years of age. Swept up in the vigorous social and cultural milieu of the era following the Harlem Renaissance in the 1920s,[2] Lawrence drew upon Harlem scenes and black history for his subjects, portraying the lives and aspirations of black Americans.

Despite the poverty of the Depression, energies of the Harlem Renaissance persisted in the community into the 1930s, and Harlem continued to be a national hub of cultural renewal. The community overflowed with an exciting accumulation of talent and ideas. By 1936, Lawrence had established work space in the studio of painter Charles Alston at 306 West 141st Street—the renowned "306" studio that was a gathering place for people in the arts.[3] There Lawrence met and learned from such black intellectuals as philosopher Alain Locke, writers Langston Hughes and Claude McKay, and painter Aaron Douglas.

Lawrence's first paintings assumed the character of Social Realism, a popular style of the 1930s. His earliest works date from around 1936 and were typically interior scenes or outdoor street views of Harlem activity. He was primarily influenced by the other community artists, such as Charles Alston, sculptor Augusta Savage, and sculptor Henry Bannarn, who all encouraged him and inspired him by their interest in themes of ethnic origin and social injustice.

At the Harlem Art Workshops, Lawrence was trained in the work of the old masters, such as Giotto, and modern masters such as Vincent van Gogh, Paul Cézanne, and Henri Matisse. He became impressed with the work of Pieter Breughel the Elder, the sixteenth century Flemish painter whose witty, narrative, and often allegorical scenes of peasant life were rendered in a flat, colorful, hard-edged manner that appealed to Lawrence. He studied the expressive prints of Honoré Daumier, Käthe Kollwitz, and Francisco Goya, especially Goya's *The Disasters of War* etching series of 1810, and was captivated by their dramatic images. He was drawn to the pungent political and social satire of the German Expressionist George Grosz. He was particularly influenced by the art of the Mexican muralists José Clemente Orozco, Diego Rivera, and David Alfaro Siqueiros, and was attracted to their artistic involvement with native heritage and the overthrow of oppression.

As a teenager, Lawrence spent much time at the Metropolitan Museum, studying the techniques of Renaissance panel painters such as Crivelli and Botticelli. He also became increasingly aware of artists who worked in various modes of abstraction, among them Arthur Dove, Charles Sheeler, and Giorgio de Chirico. And he shared the Harlem community's interest in African art and Africanism.

Through these combined influences, Lawrence arrived at a style that today retains much of its original qualities. His simplified forms are presented through representational imagery; he uses water-base media

FIGURE 1 *Jacob Lawrence, 1941, soon after he completed the* Frederick Douglass *and* Harriet Tubman *series. Photo by Carl Van Vechten. Courtesy of the Beinecke Rare Book and Manuscript Library, Yale University, and the Estate of Carl Van Vechten, Joseph Solomon, Executor.*

applied in vivid color. His concerns remain those of everyday reality, the dignity of the poor, and all efforts to enhance the human condition.

A distinctive feature of Lawrence's work is his use of the series format to render narrative content.[4] He was inspired to adopt this approach by the Harlem community's interest in the stories of early black leaders, as well as by his own interest in and his reading about the struggles and deep convictions of these legendary figures.

In 1937–38, Jacob Lawrence painted *Toussaint L'Ouverture*, his first historical series. Its subject was

the Haitian slave who led his country to freedom from French rule and whose efforts culminated in the founding of the Republic of Haiti, the first black Western republic, in the early nineteenth century. Lawrence's innumerable hours of research on Toussaint in the Schomburg Collection documents at the local public library led him toward a literary approach to his subject.[5] Feeling that a single painting could not do justice to the saga he wished to portray, he chose the series format and created a sequence of forty-one paintings.

Because the leaders of the Harlem community were engaged in an articulate search for cultural identity, Lawrence was inclined to develop narrative and thematic modes in his art to communicate the black experience clearly and effectively. He was aware of the narrative serial tradition in the history of art, ranging from Egyptian and medieval wall painting to contemporary Mexican mural cycles. In addition, painters on the Mural Division of the WPA Federal Art Project in Harlem were producing wall paintings of sequential narrative sections throughout the community in the 1930s. Charles Alston directed the mural activity from the "306" studio, and in 1937 he created a pair of narrative murals for the Harlem hospital. For Lawrence, the serial sequence, rather than an individual work, could better convey the range of emotion and ideas in the great stories he wished to tell.[6]

Through historical narrative, Lawrence was able to take his art beyond local genre and the confines of the community and to celebrate African-American history and its significant figures. Lawrence's statement offered as the epigraph for this chapter, while made fifty years ago, remains his strongest verbal expression of artistic purpose. It also indicates the depth of his knowledge about these historic figures and the extent to which they have informed his philosophy.

Jacob Lawrence produced the *Frederick Douglass* and *Harriet Tubman* series between 1938 and 1940. He painted them in casein tempera on gessoed hardboard panels measuring 12 by 17⅞ inches. The paintings of each series form a narrative; each panel depicts a significant episode in the life of the hero and is accompanied by a numbered descriptive caption. The *Frederick Douglass* series is comprised of thirty-two panels, and the *Harriet Tubman* series of thirty-one panels.[7]

When he began work on the first of these two series, Lawrence had never been to the South, the setting of much of these series' imagery, but his parents had been part of the Great Migration of African Americans that surged around 1910–16 and continued into the 1940s, drawing blacks from the southern states and the Caribbean islands to work and social opportunities in the industrial cities of the North. Lawrence's parents, both southerners, brought with them an intimate knowledge of tales of the horrors and tribulations of slavery that their own parents and grandparents had endured.

Frederick Douglass and Harriet Tubman were legends in Harlem when Lawrence was growing up. Douglass had died in 1895 and Harriet Tubman in 1913; both had lived in New York state. Their exploits and ideas had been reported widely in the newspapers, and their accomplishments were still fresh in the minds of many. As the spirit of black consciousness grew during the Harlem Renaissance and the years immediately following, such inspiring figures as Douglass and Tubman became sources of racial pride. Lawrence recalls, "People would speak of these things on the street. I was encouraged by the community to do [narrative] works of this kind; they were interested in them."[8]

The *Frederick Douglass* and *Harriet Tubman* series are unique in Lawrence's body of work for several reasons. The two series, in appearance quite different from the rest of Lawrence's work, form a pair thematically and visually. The artist pursues subjects who are related by their history, social condition, and race. Both share the qualities of determination and the will, in the face of all odds, to free their minds and spirits as well as their bodies from bondage. Both Douglass and Tubman were major figures in the antislavery cause; they are male and female counterparts representing the epitome of black American history. The epic common to their history as Americans is the Civil War, a conflict that destroyed the land and institutions of their enslavement and exile, but that also forced American blacks to establish new homes in the North in a kind of second exile.

Each series depicts personal symbolic journeys. Frederick Douglass cut a path from ignorance to learning and self-knowledge; he traveled from being a pawn of the circumstances of his birth to independence, responsibility, and action. Harriet Tubman journeyed from slavery to a freedom that transformed her into the mythical figure of a New World Moses acting out her role against the ancient and powerful symbolic resonance of the enslaved Jews of the Old Testament, their exile and wandering in the wilderness, and their eventual entry, after trials and privation, to a new homeland and the condition of freedom.

Aesthetically, the paintings of the two series are related through their small size and raw, painterly technique. A particularly unifying element is the rhythm established by the repeated umbers and greens in the panels of the two series—colors that become symbolic allusions to the soil to which these two onetime slaves were so inextricably tied.

Rooted in the black experience, Jacob Lawrence's art has demonstrated a persistent concern with the theme of human struggle. In the *Frederick Douglass* and *Harriet Tubman* series, Lawrence's boldly expressive style projects a compelling portrayal of the universal human story.

[Frederick Douglass] should be a famous name in American history—placed beside the names of Jefferson and Lincoln. Yet only recently has it been rescued from the oblivion to which it was assigned by our historiography.

Philip Foner, 1950

2
The *Frederick Douglass* Series (1938–39)

THE *Frederick Douglass* series presents the life of this Maryland slave who escaped servitude and rose to greatness as an abolitionist lecturer and writer, newspaper publisher and editor, and diplomat.

Frederick Douglass was born in 1818 in Tuckahoe, Talbot County, on the eastern shore of Maryland, the son of a white father whose identity he never knew and an enslaved mother from whom he was separated in infancy.[1] The boy soon experienced the hardships and cruelty of slavery. At age eight, he was sent to Baltimore to work as a houseboy, which proved a lucky turn of events. For the first time in his life, the young Douglass was neither brutalized nor hungry, and his new mistress taught him to read.

In 1833, Douglass was returned to Talbot County as a plantation laborer. Because of his rebellious nature, he was soon sent to a so-called "slave breaker" (a man whose function was to destroy the spirit of noncompliant slaves), who was unable to crush him physically or spiritually. After an attempt to escape, Douglass was again sent to Baltimore, this time to work in the shipyards. He finally succeeded in escaping in 1838 and made his way to New York City. There he married Anna Murray, a free black woman he had met in Baltimore; they eventually had five children. The young couple moved to New Bedford, Massachusetts, where Douglass worked at odd jobs for four years. Here Douglass, born Frederick Augustus Washington Bailey, adopted a new surname to evade capture.

While attending an abolitionist meeting in Nantucket in 1841, Douglass was asked to speak of his experience as a slave and he captivated the audience. He soon became a full-time lecturer for the Massachusetts Anti-Slavery Society and traveled with William Lloyd Garrison and Wendell Phillips. He became a famous antislavery orator, and for over fifty years drew huge crowds to hear his powerful presentations. "In listening to him," wrote a contemporary, "your whole soul is fired, every nerve is strung—every faculty you possess is ready to perform at a moment's bidding."[2]

In 1845, Douglass published a narrative of his life, which revealed facts about his origins, his identity, and his current whereabouts. Because escaped slaves were considered chattel under the law, they could be legally captured by owners and even in the free states were legally subject to being returned into slavery. Details in the *Narrative* made Douglass vulnerable to capture.[3] To avoid this disaster he fled to England, where he traveled and lectured on the evils of slavery.[4]

He returned to the United States in 1847 after some English Quaker abolitionists he met abroad purchased his freedom for £150 sterling. Douglass then settled in Rochester, New York, and established a weekly abolitionist newspaper, *The North Star*, with funds given him by British sympathizers. He published the paper for sixteen years; it became an effective political vehicle for reform.

Douglass continued to speak out against slavery until the Emancipation Proclamation of President Lincoln eventually made such activity unnecessary. In addition to his public oratory and writing, Douglass was a major figure on the Underground Railroad, the clandestine network established to aid slaves fleeing from the South to northern states and territories and Canada. He was the "superintendent" of the Rochester area of this network, and his house was the headquarters of the Rochester "station," one of the northernmost stops on the Underground Railroad's eastern route before Canada.

Douglass was also a friend and confidant of John Brown. Brown consulted Douglass about his plan to seize the federal arsenal at Harper's Ferry, Virginia, and invited Douglass to participate in the October 1859 raid. Although he was not present, Douglass was indicted for being associated with the attack, and he again took refuge in England until the investigation lost impetus.

The Civil War began in 1861, and Douglass became

a powerful voice advocating the arming of blacks for the Union Army. He had several interviews with President Lincoln on the conduct of the war, and he assisted in recruiting two black regiments in Massachusetts, in which two of his sons fought.

After the war, Douglass worked diligently for freedmen's rights, to ensure that newly free blacks would have their proper place in society. For over twenty years, he led a distinguished political life. He was appointed U.S. marshal for the District of Columbia by President Rutherford B. Hayes in 1877, the first black to be assigned to that high office. In 1881, President James A. Garfield made him recorder of deeds for the District of Columbia. In 1891, President Benjamin Harrison appointed him minister-resident and consul-general to the Republic of Haiti and chargé d'affaires to Santo Domingo, the capital of the Dominican Republic.

Douglass was also one of the first advocates of equal rights for women; in 1848, he attended the Seneca Falls Convention in New York, the first women's rights convention in the United States. And he was an active and highly effective speaker for temperance.

In 1882, Douglass's first wife died, and in 1884 he married Helen Pitts, a white woman from Rochester, who was born in Rochester but had lived for many years in Washington, D.C., and had been a clerk in Douglass's Recorder of Deeds office. He was strongly criticized for this marriage by both whites and blacks. In 1886 and 1887, the Douglasses traveled to England, Europe, and Egypt. Frederick Douglass died of a heart attack in February 1895 in his home in the Anacostia section of Washington, D.C., after attending a women's rights meeting.[5]

Jacob Lawrence divided the *Frederick Douglass* series into three parts, reflecting Douglass's autobiography: The Slave, The Fugitive, and The Free Man.[6] The paintings and their captions are intimately connected.

The captions are adapted from sources Lawrence assimilated in his research in the Schomburg Collection materials—primarily Frederick Douglass's autobiography (the 1845 and 1881 versions).

The first panel of the series is a Maryland landscape with a provocative caption that is loosely taken from Douglass's own words in the opening pages of his first autobiographical account:

In Talbot County, eastern shore, state of Maryland, in a thinly populated worn-out district, inhabited by a white population of the lowest order, among slaves who in point of ignorance were fully in accord with their surroundings—it was here that Frederick Douglass was born and spent the first years of his childhood—February 1818.

In panel 1, the artist assumes a distant view of a broad landscape, suggesting an impression of the vast holdings of the plantation owner, Colonel Edward Lloyd. Figures of the slaves, busy at work, are depicted against this backdrop; children play among the rude cabins of the slave quarters. A counterpoint to the apparent harmony of the scene is offered by the dark trees spreading spiky, angular limbs that both separate and embrace the vignettes of the composition.

In the widely varied paintings of the series, the compositions are spare but forceful. Bold, dark color schemes and simple designs are used to enhance narrative force. As in this first panel, perspective is frequently steep, with depth achieved by overlap and stacking of forms to indicate spatial recession. Figures form silhouettes of color; subordinate forms are carefully selected by the artist to support narrative thrust. Against an umber background, patches of bright, pure hues punctuate the composition.

In the *Frederick Douglass* series, Lawrence turned to a new medium, casein tempera.[7] He mixed his own paint from ground pigment, a milk protein solution, and ammonia (a preservative). He applied the paint to hardboard panels layered with gesso, which creates a hard, chalky white absorbent surface that causes paint to dry quickly; the artist must paint over an area if he wishes to make changes, thus building up color.

The young Frederick Douglass was placed with his grandmother to be reared with the other slave children in her cabin on the edge of the plantation, because his mother had been hired out. In panel 2, Douglass's mother steals a moment with him in a slave cabin, after making the twelve-mile journey on foot to visit him at night. The cabin walls assume the character of a stage backdrop; they are askew, creating a sense of tension. Strong diagonals and a wide-angle perspective give the work a disorienting motion, as if the house were about to collapse from its own conflicting energies in a world of chaos and imminent change. The mother's red dress provides focus as the two huddle before a candle. The ochre of the clay cabin floor flows out the door, continuous with the landscape.[8]

Lawrence's early paintings have a naive, "primitive" look because his forms are flat and simplified, and figures and objects appear to float in space. Close scrutiny of this panel reveals Lawrence's method: in his design, the artist has pared content to its essential core and reduced gestures to quickly grasped movements. In this economy and selectiveness, his simplicity fulfills his goal of establishing clarity of message. The artist's persistent limited color preference is evident: the primary colors (red, yellow, and blue), some secondary colors (especially green here), and black and white. Lawrence considers a narrow palette more challenging; he enjoys mixing his own colors and feels that working with so few elements forces him to have to be more inventive.[9]

In painting his series, Lawrence applied an unusual system. From his research, he first selected written passages that stimulated active images in his mind. He then created drawings that were either visual equivalents of or complements to the captions' text, with the imagery and captions becoming interdependent. In the pencil underdrawings, he drew a freehand "frame" around the area for each image, about three-eighths inch from the edge of the gessoed panel. He then completed all of the drawings for a series and laid them out in sequence.

Instead of completing each painting in order, he mixed a color and filled the areas in each panel where that color was to appear, using darker colors first. Repeating this procedure for each color, he thus worked on all the panels together to obtain consistency of color throughout the entire series. This procedure also evinces the extraordinary intellectual as well as artistic coherence of Lawrence's view of the series as a whole. The captions often go farther than simple description, to give details beyond the imagery of each painting, thus expanding the meaning of each work in space and time as well as in emotional scope.[10]

Frederick Douglass was five or six when he was taken from his grandmother to work at the house of Colonel Lloyd's chief agent and slave master, Captain Anthony, on the Lloyd estate. Panel 3 deals with the cruelties of the slave system and depicts Douglass's first experience seeing a woman flogged; she may have been a relative of his.[11] A group of slave children watch fearfully; with characteristic mordant wit, Lawrence depicts the young Douglass's eyes open wide with fright, lending focus. Because Lawrence preferred to use predominantly dark, somber colors in these two series, he developed a system of using thin relief lines (of white, green, or blue) around certain dark shapes that abut other dark areas, seen here in the woman's fingers as her hand grasps the trunk of the tree. Douglass can be identified in the panels throughout the series because of his relatively lighter skin color.

Panels 4 and 5 contrast with irony the living conditions of slave and master. In panel 4, the artist shows that many slaves sleep in a one-room cabin, with no beds and few blankets, on the clay floor. Some try to keep warm with flour sacks over their feet, and others put their feet toward the hearth. In a light-hearted touch, Lawrence paints pairs of feet extending into the picture at the lower edge. Colorful baskets woven by the slaves double as work baskets and baby beds. Sprouting from the dirt floor of the slave cabin is a sturdy red flower, a recurrent symbol of hope in both the *Douglass* and *Tubman* series.

The luxury of the master's sleeping quarters (panel 5), with an elevated perspective, seems claustrophobic: the space is filled with a richly draped canopy bed and a baby's elaborate crib. Lawrence's interest in boldly colored geometric pattern is evident.[12]

Douglass was sent to Baltimore in 1826 to work in the house of Hugh Auld, Captain Anthony's son-in-law; his duty was to take care of Tommy, the young son of the household. In panel 6, young Douglass hides behind Sophia Auld's chair while she is being severely chastised by her husband for teaching the boy to read.[13] The frontal composition is divided into geometric areas.

Paintings 7 and 8 focus on Douglass's extraordinary efforts to educate himself. He succeeds in getting his white friends to share what they have learned in school. In panel 7, the boys study at night in a stark area with broom and coal buckets, and in panel 8, Douglass reads alone at a high trestle table near a woodburning stove after his work is done.[14] In his autobiography, Douglass makes the point that reading was a revelation to him: it opened his mind to truth, and he was never again able to tolerate the condition of slavery. This was the turning point in his life and kindled his yearning for freedom.[15] In panels 7 and 8, the interior scenes are rendered with the ochre hues and diagonals of panel 2, but here they begin to assume a more rational order and perspective.

The texture of the brushwork, particularly evident in the green floor of panel 7, enlivens the painting. In the *Frederick Douglass* and *Harriet Tubman* series, the paint is applied thinly, and frequently the underdraw-

ing is still visible. Much of the appeal of the panels lies in the textural freshness of the application of the paint, a new feature in these series: the viewer can discern exactly how the artist created each area. Still evident are the unrefined brushstrokes following form and creating line and movement within form.

Frederick Douglass was sent back to live at St. Michaels, Maryland, in 1833 to work for Thomas Auld of the Anthony family. Plantation life and the hardships Douglass and others endured are rendered in panels 9 though 13. Many scenes of the series are composed in a shallow space, close up and without a horizon, which creates focus and clarity of content. In panel 9, a Sunday school meeting of the slaves is broken up by a vicious mob that fears they might be plotting escape.[16]

In panel 10, Douglass gains great emotional strength from successfully fighting off his cruel overseer, Mr. Covey. The fateful confrontation took place in a stable; tack and farrier equipment fill the picture. Douglass speaks in his autobiography of his body and spirit being broken and his hope extinguished at the cruel hands of Covey until he was inspired to fight back.[17]

In panel 11, the slaves are manipulated into drunkenness: the young Douglass sits against the wall, bewildered. A man lying on the floor forms a graceful silhouette elegantly outlined in green.[18] Panel 12 portrays Douglass and a group conspiring to escape at night. Douglass shares with his co-conspirators what he had learned from *The Columbian Orator*, "with its eloquent orations and spicy dialogues denouncing oppression," to help inspire them. "I here began my public speaking," he said.[19] Panel 13 shows the three betrayed slaves being taken away to jail in chains.

After the unsuccessful escape, in 1836 Douglass was again sent to Hugh Auld's home in Baltimore, where he was assigned to work in the shipyards of a man named William Gardiner. In panel 14, an exciting composition, the viewer's position is the depths of the hold of a great ship: the caulkers climb up to work on the vast wooden hull that towers over them. Douglass is at the top of the ladder, reaching out with his caulking tool. A narrow sliver of sky is visible.[20]

In a reflection typical of Douglass's profound insight into the condition of slavery, he articulated in his autobiography his philosophy about giving up one's earnings to a master:

To make a contented slave, you must first make a thoughtless one. It is necessary to darken his moral and mental vision, and, as far as possible to annihilate his power of reason. The man who takes his earnings must be able to convince him that he has a perfect right to do so.[21]

PART II of the series, The Fugitive, begins with Douglass's escape (panel 15). Douglass had borrowed "sailor's protection papers" from a free black sailor; dressed in sailor garb, he fled Baltimore by train. The composition is difficult to read and is filled with tension: the images, seen from a viewpoint above the train, seem to be climbing the picture plane in a steeply tipped perspective. Railroad cars curve around the lower edge. Field workers are visible beyond the train and vertical trees balance the emphatic diagonal of the train.[22]

Panel 16 refers to Douglass's first years in the North. His initial destination was New York City, where he was taken in by an abolitionist. He then sent for his fiancée in Baltimore, and they were married.[23] They quickly moved on to New Bedford, Massachusetts, where, it was believed, he would be safer. He could not find caulking work because of prejudice against color among white caulkers,[24] so he had to take whatever work was available. The panel depicts Douglass on the docks shoveling coal, bending vigorously to the hard, dirty work. The bow of a ship, seen from below, looms over the pilings of the pier, while two men sit leisurely watching the workers. The implied movement of the birds in the sky is a typical counterpoint to the static angularities of the composition.

Soon after arriving in New Bedford, Douglass began subscribing to the antislavery weekly *The Liberator*, edited by William Lloyd Garrison. This paper, as Douglass noted, forever changed his life:

From this time I was brought into contact with the mind of Mr. Garrison, and his paper took a place in my heart second only to the Bible. It detested slavery, and made no truce with the traffickers in the bodies and souls of men. It preached human brotherhood; it exposed hypocrisy and wickedness in high places; it denounced oppression, and with all the solemnity of "thus saith the Lord," demanded the complete emancipation of my race. I loved this paper and its editor.[25]

Douglass regularly attended the antislavery meetings held in New Bedford, and his heart set to pounding at the exciting words he heard. He became increasingly impressed with Garrison's commitment against slavery and prejudice and his simple Christian earnestness. In panel 17, Garrison's speech takes place in a church, the altarpiece behind him reinforcing the sense of his religious ardor. In the altarpiece, Lawrence has depicted Christ enveloped in the scarlet robe he wore just before his death, emblematic of his suffering and sacrifice. The artist makes use of a pattern of geometrical but expressive back views of figures in this panel, recalling the work of the Renaissance master Giotto, as well as that of Orozco.

Douglass's career as an abolitionist speaker began when he attended a large antislavery convention on Nantucket, which had been organized by Garrison and his friends in the summer of 1841. He was asked to speak of his experiences as a slave and from then on became an enthusiastic agent in the Massachusetts Anti-Slavery Society. People proved eager to hear his story. In panel 18, the artist employs a traditional pyramidal design, with Douglass at its apex gesturing dramatically. Through the sweep of Douglass's glance

FIGURE 2 *Frederick Douglass, c. 1855. Photograph courtesy of the Schomburg Center for Research in Black Culture, New York Public Library.*

and his coattail, the viewer's eye is directed downward to the figure of a small child at the side, standing with legs apart in a pugnacious pose. This kind of witty, human touch is characteristic of Lawrence's outlook, reflecting his sense of humor and his intention not to allow Douglass to take himself too seriously.

Historian Benjamin Quarles's description of Douglass's appearance and oratorial impact gives us insight into the magnetism of this man:

Favorably endowed in physique, Douglass had the initial advantage of looking like a person destined for prominence. There was a dramatic quality in his very appearance—his imposing figure, his deep-set flashing eyes and well-formed nose, and the mass of hair crowning his head. An exceptional platform speaker, he had a voice created for public address in premicrophone America. In speaking he was capable of various degrees of light and shade, his powerful tones hinting at a readiness to overcome faulty acoustics. His rich baritone gave an emotional vitality to every sentence.[26]

Early photographs of Douglass reveal that he was indeed an unusually robust-looking man with a commanding presence, his appearance matching his exploits.

Douglass was considered an important component of the 1843 series of abolitionist conventions in the Northern states because his first-hand accounts of slavery were powerfully persuasive. When an irate mob of pro-slavery adherents attacked him and his fellow speakers in Pendleton, Indiana (panel 19), Douglass was left unconscious and with a broken hand; the bones were never set properly and he lost its full strength and dexterity.[27] The incident is set forth in a dynamic composition filled with angular diagonal stresses. Douglass's feet extend elegantly, strongly reminiscent of this feature in the 1913 figural street scenes of German Expressionist Ernst Ludwig Kirchner, whose work Lawrence knows. The artist here creates a portrait of Douglass, his thick hair parted and smoothed down.

Douglass was so articulate and well-spoken an orator that some people doubted he had ever been a slave. These spreading feelings that he was an impostor induced him to write his first autobiography in 1844 to clear up the matter by publishing the facts—names, places, dates—of his slavery experience. These revelations put him at risk of being returned to slavery, and, accompanied by a friend from Massachusetts, Douglass sought refuge in Britain from 1845 to 1847.[28]

Panel 20 shows Douglass's audience at the time of his speech at the World's Temperance Convention in London in 1846, from his viewpoint at the lectern.[29] There are several humorous touches: the hall is filled with religious leaders from all over the world. Some, from the slave-holding states in America, are disturbed at his words; the artist depicts three of them with their hands over their ears. The center aisle implies emphatic linear perspective, interrupted only by one listener's foot sticking out, and yet there is no diminution in the faces as the perspective recedes, enhancing the flatness and steepness of the picture plane and creating a tension that plays against the pattern of the repeated heads. Despite the static premise of seated figures, Lawrence conveys the crowd's restlessness and animation through posture and facial expression; members of the audience talk to each other, look away, drape their arms over seat backs. This panel, in reversing the back viewpoint of panel 17, reinforces an awareness that Douglass has now become the speaker to whom audiences look for guidance. Curiously, in the caption for panel 20, Lawrence does not mention the reason Douglass went to Britain: to avoid capture after publishing his autobiography.

During his stay in Britain, in 1846 two Quaker Englishwomen sent Captain Auld in Maryland a payment for Douglass's freedom. With the papers of his manumission in his possession, he could return safely to the United States.[30] Panel 21 is the cardinal piece of the series, portraying Douglass seated at his desk, working as editor of *The North Star*. Douglass established the newspaper with $2,500 given to him by British friends so that he could start a paper advocating the interests of his "enslaved and oppressed people."[31] In this interior scene, the characteristic dramatically tipped space is a persistent reference to the work of such modernists as de Chirico and Sheeler, of whose work Lawrence was aware. An umber background is scattered with angular patches of bright, pure color. The subordinate forms are selected by the artist to emphasize the writing and reference materials used by Douglass. Douglass's accomplishments in writing and lecturing were amazing, as he was completely self-educated. His autobiography reveals that he knew history and literature: he frequently mentions significant historical figures and he often quotes from Shakespeare.

Douglass relished his role in the Underground Railroad. His work as stationmaster and conductor in Rochester was extremely dangerous, putting him at risk of fine and imprisonment. But Douglass enjoyed "hitting that old enemy [slavery] some telling blows." He received fugitives and lodged and fed them until he could raise enough money to send them on to St. Catharines, Ontario, Canada, a place of refuge in "the Queen's Dominions." Despite the risk, Douglass states: "I never did more congenial, attractive, fascinating, and satisfactory work. . . . It was like an attempt to bail out the ocean with a teaspoon, but . . . [it] brought to my heart unspeakable joy."[32] Douglass would often come home to find fugitives waiting on his doorstep. In panel 22, Lawrence illustrates just such an incident.[33] A frontal tableau, the simple composition presents the waiting group as Douglass encountered them: the eleven adults and children are lined up across the picture plane, vulnerable, scared, and hopeful.

Panels 23 and 24 deal with the relationship of Frederick Douglass and the great abolitionist John Brown. Brown went to his death convinced that he had a divine mission to overthrow black slavery in America. The two first met at Brown's house in Springfield, Massachusetts, in 1847; Douglass dined with him and his family, and then stayed well into the next day, talking about antislavery goals. John Brown denounced slavery and discussed his ideas about abolishing the system, and Douglass listened eagerly and was impressed with Brown's strong will, "stern truth, and solid purpose."[34]

Panel 23 is an unusual close-up portrait of the two men: Douglass is about thirty years old at the time, and John Brown is about fifty. The scene focuses on the face of the obsessed Brown. Old photos indicate Lawrence's treatment of Brown is relatively accurate: a haggard man with a long, narrow head and unkempt white hair that grew low on his forehead, Brown looked much like a vision of an Old Testament prophet.

Eleven years later, in 1858, as Douglass's house guest

in Rochester, Brown drafted a constitution for his revolutionary organization. In panel 24, John Brown and Frederick Douglass debate the wisdom of Brown's plan to seize the federal arsenal at Harper's Ferry and arm his freedom soldiers. The centrally placed crucifix is symbolic of both men's adherence to God's guidance in their struggle. Yet Brown was a fanatic. A contemporary account describes him:

He was very pious and had been deeply impressed for years with the story of Gideon, believing that he, with a handful of men, could strike down slavery.[35]

In his passion, John Brown gestures assertively in the painting, while Douglass listens attentively.

Just weeks before the Harper's Ferry attack, Brown asked Douglass to participate in the raid, but Douglass declined because he felt it was a doomed strategy and that there was no way for Brown's band to avoid capture. After Harper's Ferry, all associated with John Brown were indicted, even those not present in the raid; those caught were hung for treason. Knowing that he was about to be arrested because he had supplied Brown with money, men, and friendship, Douglass fled to Canada, and in November 1859 he went to England, thinking even Canada would not be safe. He returned from England six months later. Again, the artist chooses not to deal with this part of Douglass's life either in the caption or imagery, omitting reference to Douglass's second flight to England as a fugitive. In his autobiography, Douglass, perhaps feeling ambivalent about his stand on Brown's plan, examines his position at length, explaining his reasoning.[36]

After Abraham Lincoln was elected in 1860, the South rose in rebellion and secession. Many northerners sought conciliation with the South at any cost, offering assurances that the slavery system was not in jeopardy. Panel 25 illustrates one of the many attacks on abolitionist speakers during that transitional period—possibly the antiabolitionist riot in Boston on December 3, 1860, in which Douglass was a key figure. Lawrence's freeze-frame approach reads like aggressive action: outflung limbs form a harsh, slashing pattern.[37]

The rawness of Lawrence's technique enhances the emotional impact of his expressionist style. The panels of the *Frederick Douglass* and *Harriet Tubman* series are small, but many have the formal impact of much larger works. Their intimate scale invites close scrutiny, causing the viewer to become aware of the intriguing visual qualities of Lawrence's use of paint, his sureness of approach, his mastery of technique, and his compelling content.

A major issue of the Civil War was the question of participation of blacks in Union forces. There was resistance to arming blacks to fight, although they were allowed to serve first as waiters, then laborers, and finally as soldiers. Douglass firmly believed that the war would end slavery, and he appealed to all blacks to enlist. Panel 26, crossed bayonets standing on a bleak, dark hill, is a composition symbolic of the country at war.[38]

Governor Andrew of Massachusetts assured Frederick Douglass that black enlisted men would be treated justly and fairly, receiving equal pay and promotions, but it was soon evident that this was not the case. Douglass fought to rectify this condition through his writings and political contacts. In July 1863, he went to Washington, D.C., to present his complaints to President Lincoln. Panel 27 presents the allegorical sculpted figure of *Freedom*, which stands atop the Capitol dome silhouetted against the sky, her liberty cap a plumed helmet. Douglass's interview with Lincoln left him with even greater determination to fight for the participation and equal treatment of black Union troops.[39]

The passing of the Proclamation of Emancipation on January 1, 1863, cooled the enthusiasm of those northerners who did not support a war of abolition, and led to violence in many northern cities. A riot in New York in July of that year (panel 28) lasted for three days and nights and was directed at all blacks and their friends. People hid wherever they could. The painting reveals an apprehensive group; a baby sleeps in the familiar woven basket. The father shields the rest of the family as he peers into the night from their place of refuge. In the corner springs the red flower indicating hope.[40]

In setting up his thematic progression of the *Frederick Douglass* series, Lawrence emphasizes that each step forward in the struggle encountered much resistance (riots, mobs, mistreatment) among the populace. Douglass's fight, as one man against so many, is even more poignant when one recalls that the South, with its slavery-based economy, stood to lose its entire economic armature. Throughout his life, Douglass toiled against such seemingly insurmountable odds with resilience and thoughtful determination.

PART III of the series, The Free Man, is comprised of four panels (29 through 32). On December 18, 1865, the Thirteenth Amendment to the Constitution was passed, abolishing slavery. With Douglass's greatest battle won, the artist brings the series to a close.

After the Civil War, Douglass turned his efforts toward ensuring freedmen's rights. Panel 29 is an outdoor tableau depicting the newly freed slaves heading into an unknown world, driven off by southern hostility. The forest is a canopy of sharply pointed trees towering ominously over the throng. An epic grandeur is achieved by the distance assumed by the artist.[41]

There was much opposition to Douglass's appointment as U.S. marshal of the District of Columbia, a position that included attending the president at the executive mansion and formally introducing guests to him on official occasions. In panel 30, Douglass is seated in his office. He is older now, and his magnificent leonine head fills the picture, as he attends to his

FIGURE 3 *Frederick Douglass, c. 1885. Photograph courtesy of the Schomburg Center for Research in Black Culture, New York Public Library.*

duties of voice and pen. The artist uses a delicate combination of colors in the hair and on the hand; green, yellow, and blue are subtly blended. Lawrence adds a touch of elegance, a blue cufflink. For this painting and its caption, the artist combines the visual image of Douglass the dedicated public figure, with the words of Douglass the wry realist.[42]

Many blacks fled from the South, hoping for a new life elsewhere. Douglass opposed this exodus, maintaining that freedmen should not have to seek a better place but should be given better circumstances where they were. He explained:

Thousands of these poor people, traveling only so far as they had money to bear their expenses, arrived at their destinations in the extremest destitution. . . . Their tales of woe were such as to move a heart much less sensitive to human suffering than mine.[43]

One such group is rendered in panel 31. To capture movement, Lawrence, like Orozco, presents repeated, simplified striding figures that lean forward, moving from right to left—a compositional device Lawrence frequently favors. They press forward eagerly, with wide strides, carrying their meager belongings. The line of birds in the sky moves northward with them, lending direction and motion to the picture.

In the late 1870s, Frederick Douglass visited St. Michaels, Talbot County, his early home. It was a moving experience. In a chapter entitled "Time Makes All Things Even" in his autobiography, Douglass described his visit with his former master, Captain Thomas Auld, who was over 80 years of age and on his deathbed. He spoke of how they put aside past grievances and distinctions and had a friendly conversation. Douglass was touched when Auld admitted to him that "had I been in your place I should have done as you did."[44] The interview was a moment of emotional resolution for Douglass.

Two years later, he also visited Colonel Lloyd's plantation in Easton, which he had not seen since he had left in 1825 at age eight, and he was welcomed by Lloyd's great-grandson. Panel 32, the final work of the series, alludes to Douglass's return to Maryland in an allegorical manner. A solitary flag billows gracefully, its staff plunged into the Maryland soil, emblematic of the contribution Douglass and many others made to the cause of freedom in an evolving America. Promise and hope are insinuated by the banner, the broad streaming cloud, and the single vigorous flower.

FREDERICK DOUGLASS'S life continued for many more years beyond the narrative scope of Jacob Lawrence's series and included many significant accomplishments, but these apparently were not part of Douglass's central purpose. Taking his cue from Frederick Douglass's own approach in his writings, Lawrence omits many personal and extraneous details that might have had tangential interest. For example, Douglass barely mentions his family in his autobiog-

raphies, and Lawrence also leaves them out of the series, choosing rather to communicate Douglass's emphasis on the profound universal issues of human freedom and dignity.

It is significant that although the series is not a full biography, Lawrence follows Douglass's autobiographical accounts closely in the events he selects. In his conceptualization, Lawrence is clearly intent on illustrating Frederick Douglass's own story. In the 1930s, Douglass's name and accomplishments were not widely known in this country. In 1950, in a view foreshadowed by Jacob Lawrence, historian Philip Foner wrote about the importance of disseminating Douglass's writings:

Here is the clearest articulation of discontent, protest, militant action, and hope of the American Negro. Here one of the most brilliant minds of his time, constantly responsive to the great forces of his day, analyzes every important issue confronting the Negro and the American people generally during fifty crucial years in our history. Here are the eloquent words and penetrating thoughts that exerted a decisive influence on the course of national affairs for half a century and moved countless men and women to action in behalf of freedom. Most important of all, here are the militant principles of the outstanding leader of the Negro people whose ideas have remained vital and valid down to the present day.[45]

For Lawrence, the creation of this series went beyond personal expression and became an effort to raise consciousness.

In the sequence of paintings, the relationship of caption to image is important. Suggestive of the black oral tradition, each painting illustrates and is illuminated by its narrative caption. In choosing narrative concepts for captions, Lawrence set up a balanced structure of storm and calm. The success of the sequence stems in large part from this measuring of emotion and restraint: both images and captions offer alternating extremes in content, ranging from disturbing to humorous, active to contemplative, oppressive to aggressive, symbolic to descriptive, and struggle to fulfillment. The artist is also very conscious of establishing a visual balance in the use of horizontal and vertical compositions.

The forms in Lawrence's art are basically inspired by nature but are pruned and altered in ways that become increasingly expressionistic and cubist as his early work continues. Imagery in the series is designed with a deliberate continuity of style and color. A familiar cast of characters is scattered throughout the panels. The protagonist is present in at least half of the paintings, identified by physiognomy, costume, and gestures. For example, Frederick Douglass is usually identifiable through his broad shoulders and thick mass of hair (e.g., panels 10, 19, 30) and his gestures (panels 14 and 18).

Although Lawrence could have presented the story of Frederick Douglass's life in an overwhelmingly strident way, the artist chose to reflect Douglass's philosophy about aesthetics and personal style. Douglass, as Benjamin Quarles has observed, "writes as a partisan but his indignation is always under control."[46] Furthermore, Douglass's account is full of clever irony and sardonic nuances. Lawrence, as well, tempers heavily emotional content with humor: the evils of slavery are made clear in the series, visually and in the accompanying captions, but at just the right points a leavening of wit lightens the burden for the viewer. Much of the series' success lies in Lawrence's constant projection of the human comedy behind the tragedy. His emphasis is always on constructive human potential.

Harriet Tubman's story is one of the great American sagas. We hear about Molly Pitcher, about Betsy Ross. . . . The black woman has never been included in American history.

Jacob Lawrence, 1988

3

The *Harriet Tubman* Series (1939–40)

JACOB LAWRENCE's *Harriet Tubman* series contains thirty-one narrative panels of the same size and medium as his *Frederick Douglass* series.

Harriet Tubman, like Douglass, was born a slave on the eastern shore of Maryland, around 1820.[1] One of eleven children, she began to do hard labor at the age of five. When she was about fifteen she received a head injury at the hands of an angry overseer, which left her with a dented skull and a kind of seizure that took the form of periods of sleepiness throughout the rest of her life. Always preferring field-hand work to work indoors, she developed great strength and endurance through plowing, and cutting and loading of wood. In 1844, she married John Tubman, a free black man. About 1849, Harriet escaped to freedom in Pennsylvania, guided in her flight at night by the North Star.

In the North, Harriet Tubman did domestic work, saving her earnings to serve her determination to liberate other slaves. Beginning in 1850 she returned South at least nineteen times over a period of ten years, freeing over three hundred slaves by means of the Underground Railroad. She became one of the most notorious "conductors" on the railroad and reputedly never lost a "passenger." She was able to rescue most of her brothers and sisters, as well as her parents.

Because the Fugitive Slave Law of 1850 had just been put into effect when she began her clandestine mission, it was dangerous to stop short of the Canadian border, so she took the escapees into Canada.[2]

Although Harriet Tubman could neither read nor write, her shrewdness in planning hazardous enterprises and skill in avoiding arrest were phenomenal. She was known as being fearless and able to endure any hardship. From the beginning, she was guided in her work by spiritual visions and sustained by her strong faith in God.

Harriet Tubman was a friend of Frederick Douglass and John Brown. Brown sought her counsel on his campaign against slavery in Virginia, and she recruited troops for him and obtained financial donations. She became active in abolitionist circles of the North and was known for her moving speeches at antislavery meetings. She also often spoke on behalf of women's rights.

During the Civil War, Tubman served in the Union Army as a cook, laundress, nurse, scout, and spy. After the war, she settled in Auburn, New York, and continued to work for her people, taking in the sick and homeless, and traveling to give speeches. She died in 1913.

IN THE *Harriet Tubman* series, emotional tone ranges from drama to wit, epic grandeur to intimate psychological insight. The story is introduced in the first three paintings' captions, in which the artist sets forth the conflicts and issues of the epoch—abolitionist Henry Ward Beecher's statement against slavery, Secretary of State Henry Clay's statement rationalizing slavery, and President Abraham Lincoln's insight into the fate of a divided nation.

Panel 1 portrays a group of slaves working on the plantation. The graceful, elongated black silhouettes of striding profile figures with long, slender, bare feet evoke Egyptian wall paintings, an early influence on Lawrence (he frequently visited the Egyptian collection when at the Metropolitan Museum). They also recall the murals of Harlem artist Aaron Douglas.[3] Against a background of bare earth, areas of brilliant color sparkle like inlaid jewels. The lyrical quality of this first image leaves the viewer unprepared for the strident narrative caption to the painting, a quote from Beecher:

With sweat and toil and ignorance he consumes his life, to pour the earnings into channels from which he does not drink.[4]

The cruel experience of slavery is addressed directly in panel 2, one of the most forceful compositions of the series. The truncated figure bearing scars of a whip fills the spare visual field, in posture and wounds suggesting Christ's crucifixion and agony. In the caption, by offering Clay's statement, the artist sets forth with irony one of the many justifications of the slavery system.[5]

Panel 3 depicts a cotton plant in dramatic isolation, accompanied only by the bright ever-present Southern sun. The floral beauty of the plant belies the misery attending its cultivation. The artist's focus on a single cotton plant underscores its significance as the economic mainstay of the South and its symbolic position as the justification for the institution of slavery.[6]

The artist introduces Harriet in panel 4: she is one of a group of carefree slave children leaping and tumbling. The elliptical arrangement of figures is a traditional choice, derived ultimately from classical compositions of the Three Graces and most immediately reminiscent of Henri Matisse's *The Dance* of 1910.[7] Rather than the familiar circular, rounded curves present in Matisse's rendition, however, Lawrence injects his composition with spiky, angular figural elements that enhance the underlying expressive, emotional content in this seemingly joyful image.

The assault in which Harriet received a debilitating head injury is portrayed in panel 5. The perspective is steeply tipped, creating a precarious visual environment. The young Harriet lies on the ground unconscious after being hit with a two-pound iron weight; the overseer who struck her retreats. Harriet's little shift and bare feet emphasize her vulnerability. A black snake slithers across the path: reminiscent of the serpent in the Garden of Eden, the snake conveys the idea that the slave's plantation life was not an idyll of rustic simplicity and innocence. The snake appears throughout the Tubman series, symbolic of the ever-present wickedness that stalks Harriet and all the slaves.

Panel 6, a consummate abstraction, is a night scene, a shadowy vision of slave women being whipped. Law-rence's linear, pointed forms capture dramatically the tension of the tortured women in this haunting, ghostly image. The shadows of the overseer and his whip are projected eerily, echoed by the women's supplicating hands. In this panel, the artist uses his paint in a fluid, monochromatic manner that calls to mind Chinese ink paintings.

The despair in panels 5 and 6 is counteracted by the imagery of panel 7, which focuses on Harriet cutting wood on the plantation. Splendid strength is conveyed in her now mature, massive form. Her arms and hands loom forward with emphatic presence as she bends over her task. The kerchiefed head is bowed, the features indistinct; only subtle outlines delineate the nose and an eye. Her foot peeks out elegantly from her skirt hem as her knee braces the log. In this epitome of Lawrence's gift for simple but forceful composition, the figure boldly fills the picture plane with its hulking shape, an interplay of oblique angles. Relief from the blocky, overwhelming solidity of the central form is created by feathered brushstrokes.

Lawrence's work is not an attempt at naturalism: his form is always stylized, with a dominant sense of abstraction enhanced by sureness of line. Figural distortions typical of Lawrence's style in the two series also appear, for example, in the work of Harlem artist Henry Bannarn and the Mexican muralists. Emphasis on muscularity and powerful hands and arms to symbolize courage and power is seen frequently in art of social content of the 1930s. Large hands are also a formal device in Picasso's Cubism and Neoclassicism familiar at the time. Lawrence often uses big hands to clarify points and bulk or thinness of figures to reinforce emotional tone, in a manner similar to conventions of medieval art. Artistic license notwithstanding, descriptions, photographs, and engravings of Harriet Tubman reveal that she, like Frederick Douglass, was a person of unusually strong physique.

Biographer Earl Conrad described Harriet Tubman

as about five feet tall, stocky, and very strong. She had gained strength from doing the work of an able-bodied man: her arms were heavily muscled and her hands powerful and calloused; she went shoeless in the fields. Her eyes were heavy-lidded and, even as a teenager, she began to take on the magnetic appearance that would later be described in various terms from "magnificent" to "fierce." Conrad states that "she could lift huge barrels of produce and draw a leaded stone boat like an ox."[8]

Panel 7, like panel 21 of the *Douglass* series, is the portrait of the *Tubman* series. In rendering Harriet's appearance, the artist was no doubt influenced by pictures of her and accounts of her appearance. Lawrence must have been inspired in particular by the woodcut of Harriet Tubman on the cover of Bradford's first biography of Tubman, which has been widely distributed. In this 1860s rendition, Tubman wears the striped skirt and patterned kerchief that Lawrence adopts in his painting. Conrad also confirms that Harriet wore long skirts and a colorful bandana to protect her head from the sun. (Although Conrad's accounts were written after Lawrence produced the series, they were based on the archival and photographic material available to Lawrence in the Schomburg Collection.)[9]

In panel 8, Harriet is auctioned off to the highest bidder. The artist focuses on the emotional trauma of the individual, not the event: the slave auction is presented from Harriet's viewpoint as she stands on the platform, while the buyers, with guns and whips handy, bid on human flesh. The figural composition is a traditional stable pyramid. As he frequently does, Lawrence caricatures the white person's physiognomy, taking the opportunity for wry social observation and critical comment. The buyers' thin, skeletal heads and narrowed eyes convey a sense of menace, reinforced by the barren trees nearby.

Panel 9 is a compelling antislavery statement. Heavy chains encircle the ankles of the slaves. The combined

HARRIET TUBMAN.

FIGURE 4 *Harriet Tubman, c. 1863–68, woodcut. Photograph courtesy of the Schomburg Center for Research in Black Culture, New York Public Library.*

effect of strong, graceful legs and feet and colorful clothes is one of persevering pride and hope. Harriet Tubman was subject to visions and dreams and believed in the power of prayer. She also was particularly inspired by the rebellious efforts of slaves such as Nat Turner in 1831.[10] She became haunted by a recurrent nightmare of being sold away from Maryland into the deep South, where slavery was reputed to be far more cruel, and she was seized by the compulsion to escape. She had fantasies of the land of freedom, full of "green fields and lovely flowers."[11] She quickly put these feelings into action when she heard a rumor that she and two of her brothers were soon going to be sent South.

Tubman was in her late twenties when she escaped at night, severing her bondage forever, and leaving her husband behind. Panels 10 through 12 are devoted to her first journey North. Her two brothers started out with her but became afraid and soon turned back, so she continued alone. All three paintings depict broad landscapes and the night skies under which the solitary Harriet journeyed toward safety. She went with no money, through territory unknown to her, traveling by night and hiding by day.[12] She used slave lore to help locate landmarks, and sometimes she received food and shelter from sympathetic people.

In panel 10, Harriet climbs over a steep rise, her hand extended to pull herself up. The North Star is overhead, and the black snake lurks. She carries a few belongings in a red satchel, and her eyes are wide with fear. An uneven landscape with quaking trees and an energized sky with swirling clouds and big yellow stars recall Van Gogh's *Starry Night* (1889), a painting familiar to Lawrence.

The sky and stars are important elements in the *Harriet Tubman* series: the night sky is her constant canopy on her many Underground Railroad trips, and the stars helped light her way. The artist renders the stars expressionistically in a hasty, childlike manner. They are drawn continuously, as if connecting five dots, with dabs of yellow added afterward. Harriet wears a white robe, an aesthetic and symbolic choice by the artist; Lawrence says that he probably chose white for her robe to create high contrast with the dark background and to also symbolize the purity of her mission.[13]

For the caption of panel 11, Lawrence chose the actual published reward notice for Harriet Tubman's capture; its language is indicative of the bizarre owner/slave relationship, and describes human attributes as if mere chattel were being discussed. (Harriet Tubman was also called Araminta, an African name, or Minty, as she is named in the notice.) The accompanying painting lacks any human figure. A cold, empty night scene is dominated by a flesh-colored cloud—a hand beckoning her onward to the land of freedom.

In panel 12, the figure of Harriet appears: just a white robe and a wide stride, as she bends forward. Her form is dwarfed by the vast, lonely landscape. Space recedes into infinity. The gently curved mountain evergreen trees that loom over her become anthropomorphic, friendly sheltering presences.

Panel 13 shows Harriet Tubman arriving in Pennsylvania, a free state, where she could walk about in daylight; the sun shines brightly over her. Among Northerners she remains apprehensive, hiding on the edge of the crowd. The artist portrays this frightening and disillusioning moment for Harriet with wit and compassion: her efforts to conceal herself are comical, and we observe all kinds of white people here, not just sinister Southern stereotypes.[14]

Little is known about either the circumstances of Harriet's journey North or the persons who assisted her. Panel 14 illustrates an incident in which Harriet was aided by a woman and was allowed to rest in an oddly shaped room.[15] Amid the chaotic attitude of the room's walls, reminiscent of cabin interiors in the *Douglass* series, Harriet, having trusted to Providence, calmly eats her meal in an atmosphere that evokes sacrament. She wears the now characteristic white robe that signifies her spiritual quest. As is frequently true in the series, Harriet is the only stable form in the composition. Here her profile is rendered unusually naturalistically, as the viewer is allowed to share this personal moment with Harriet. The composition recalls typical features of Picasso's work, as well as the art of Georges Braque and Paul Cézanne, in the carefully delineated fruit arrangement and the tilted cubist space. Perhaps borrowing from Giotto, Lawrence uses the medieval convention of a landscape visible through a window; here the artist renders a stark view appropriate to his sober theme.[16]

In the North, first in Philadelphia and then in Cape

May, New Jersey, Harriet Tubman was overjoyed that she could now choose her work and keep her earnings. She cooked, cleaned, scrubbed, and did laundry, saving all her income for her trips South to rescue slaves. According to Conrad, Tubman's first trip South to bring back fugitives through the Underground Railroad was in December 1850, when she rescued a sister and her sister's two children in Baltimore.[17] On her third trip South in 1851, to bring back her husband, she found that he had remarried.[18]

Panels 15 and 16 focus on bringing fugitives North. Both scenes evoke biblical stories: the Israelites wandering in the wilderness, and the wise men following the star (panel 15). Harriet Tubman and her three charges are small against the dark sky; the simple conception is enlivened by dynamic brushstrokes. A formal row of trees in panel 16 becomes the orderly backdrop for a group of hastening fugitives who press forward, their figures and knapsacks creating laterally repeated rounded forms, in the manner of Orozco (e.g., *The Soldiers*, 1926, the Museum of Modern Art). Shadows on forms become stylized design elements; the bare feet eloquently convey their plight.

The caption for panel 16 refers to William Still, whom Harriet Tubman had met in 1849 just after arriving in the North. It was through him that she gained her intimate knowledge of the Underground Railroad. Still was the chief person on the railroad in Philadelphia, which was the "Grand Central Terminal" of the eastern route. He was director of the Vigilance Committee that forwarded fugitives to New York City, a clerk in the office of the Pennsylvania Anti-Slavery Society, and was known throughout the state for his abolition work.[19]

Through the black oral tradition, Harriet Tubman became a legendary conductor on the Underground Railroad. By the turn of the nineteenth century, the two main routes of the network ran through the midwest into Canada and up the eastern seaboard to To-ronto. Tubman was one of about five hundred conductors who operated each year; most were black, being most intimately compelled by the cause but also most subject to severe reprisals. Often on the hazardous journeys, fugitives would fall to the ground exhausted, refusing to take another step. Harriet carried a gun and was known to threaten her charges with death if they would not continue, rather than risk exposure of the network by the faint-hearted.[20]

Harriet's rescue exploits became widely known. She was so skilled at eluding detection that to slave owners she seemed to appear from nowhere, only to vanish in a flash with several more fugitives. She was known as "Moses" because she led so many to freedom, but her true identity was known only to the slaves she rescued; most others thought "Moses" was a man.[21] In panel 17, Harriet appears as if a phantom charged with celestial energy and perhaps, even as Moses, inspired by God, as she swoops down on the plantation to lead more slaves to freedom in the "promised land" of the North.

Themes of oppression and bondage, flight and exile, sacrifice and endurance, and action and responsibility emerge in this series in a symbolic synthesis of Old and New Testament allegory. Harriet Tubman is depicted by Lawrence with the wiliness and single-minded determination of a Moses, the practical strength of a Martha, the grace and compassion of a Mary. Many panels depict the vast tract of the heavens or broad, sparsely populated landscapes, suggesting the scale of the cosmos in which Harriet's drama, and that of all slaves, was played out and ultimately resolved.

Panels 18 and 19 deal with the relentless search for Harriet Tubman by the plantation owners; it was presumed that she would be burned at the stake if she were caught.[22] A Massachusetts Unitarian minister, writing to his mother in 1859, called her "the greatest heroine of our age."[23] In panel 18, clawlike supernatural hands reach everywhere for Harriet, clasping even the moon. All elements have eyes, as the search for Harriet is intensified.

She eludes detection in panel 19: while slave owners gather to plot her capture beneath a snakelike whip, Harriet sneaks through an opening in the trees, protecting her charges with a melodramatic outflung arm and her cape. The composition is comprised of two groupings connected by a spatial tunnel between the trees, emphasizing how close Harriet often was to being captured. The artist contrasts the disturbing caption with the witty image.

Tubman, who usually led her fugitives into Canada, often had to brave severe Northern winter weather. Panel 20 portrays Harriet huddled with two escapees, trudging through a bleak, snowy expanse. The rounded, poignant, dumpy figures are dwarfed by nature, emphasizing their vulnerability. In Canada, the town of St. Catharines became Harriet Tubman's home between 1851 and about 1857; during these seven years she made about eleven journeys into slave country. Canada became a haven for fugitive slaves between 1850 and 1865. In 1833, Queen Victoria had proclaimed blacks free on Canadian soil.[24] St. Catharines sheltered a growing community of free blacks, the first such settlement on the American continent. One of the northernmost stops on the Underground Railroad before Canada was Rochester, New York, where Tubman would coordinate her efforts with Frederick Douglass.[25]

Harriet Tubman soon began to address gatherings of abolitionist sympathizers in the North, and was regarded as an "eloquent orator" who spoke with "quaint simplicity." Panel 21 depicts Harriet as an antislavery speaker. The steep space and interplay of diagonal stresses enhance the active scene. Eager, wide-eyed listeners are clustered at the edge of the platform. The artist's use of brushwork along opposed textural directions adds to the composition's complexity.[26]

An important station on one of Harriet's routes was the house of Thomas Garrett of Wilmington, Delaware, who gave her much assistance over the years. He is said to have aided over 2,700 fugitives and was the inspiration for Simeon Halliday in Harriet Beecher Stowe's *Uncle Tom's Cabin*. The imagery of panel 22 strikingly suggests allusions to the Old Testament themes of exile, wandering, and the sacramental table. The oldest man, at center, bowed and contemplative, could be interpreted as having a rabbinical presence; his companions bend almost reverently over their food. They are being provided for in the wilderness of their journey, and the meal has biblical overtones—an event marking the slaves' "passing over" from slavery into freedom, a commemoration similar to that which the Jews celebrate to acknowledge their release from bondage in Egypt.[27]

In the background, Harriet Tubman confers with Thomas Garrett about practical matters. The shoes on the small table refer to the fact that Garrett was proprietor of a shoe factory, and he allowed no traveler to leave his house without a new pair of shoes.[28] The shoes, a piquant detail, are an example of the artist's sense of humor, which is revealed through the lightest of touches in both the *Douglass* and *Tubman* series.

Tubman and her fugitives often sang to lift their spirits and allay fear while walking along. Panel 23 depicts a bloodhound straining at the leash, tongue hanging out and tail stiff with anticipation, an image suggested by the caption, which is part of a song Harriet and the escapees would sing as they approached the Canadian border.[29]

Harriet Tubman bought a small house and a parcel of land in Auburn, New York, from William H. Seward in 1857. There she brought her parents to live; they were over seventy years old at the time of their escape North. By this time, she was a well-known antislavery worker and speaker, even though she tried to keep out of the public eye and often concealed her identity when she spoke, in order to function effectively on the

Underground Railroad.[30] She also continued to work as a domestic to support herself and her parents, but relied on donations in the North and from abroad to finance her rescue trips South. Panel 24 shows a man's hand offering a coin to an eager Harriet Tubman who has just made a speech at an antislavery rally in the Boston area. The gesture dramatically fills the space, emblematic of the financial support of white American and English abolitionists and Harriet's effective cooperation with them.[31]

In 1858, Harriet Tubman met John Brown in Canada. He was interested in establishing contact with her because he thought she might be able to enlist the assistance of free blacks in Canada to serve in his liberation army. She agreed to work with him; he shared with her his plan to invade Virginia, and she gave him information on guerrilla tactics for the area. Brown was impressed with Harriet, immediately referring to her as "General Tubman." Harriet was moved by John Brown's dedication to the cause of her people.[32]

Panel 25 is heavily suggestive of Brown's religious fervor. The composition is cross-shaped, with the three figures arranged along the axis of the cross, and there is what appears to be the shadow of another cross on the floor in the foreground. The Bible, because of its position on the table and its bright red page edges, provides the painting with a focus. All are praying. Here, the cross-shaped design is architectonic and rational. The structure of the cross provides a support for the three struggling heroes, in contrast to the isolated anguish of the crucified figure in panel 2: the three have by this point received much support from society and their faith. Textural application of pigment in dry brushstrokes enhances the geometries of the picture plane.

Harriet Tubman's last foray to rescue slaves was a trip to Maryland in December 1860. Abraham Lincoln was elected president that fall, and South Carolina soon seceded from the Union. Harriet was pressed by friends to stay in Canada between December 1860 and the spring of 1861, for her own safety.[33] Panel 26 is a symbolic expression: a cannon is fired, representing the beginning of the Civil War. This image addresses the consequence of the act: the beginning of the war was the onset of the end of slavery in the United States. The arid landscape and denuded trees capture the sobering portents of the war. A dove of peace flies by, reminiscent of the dove sent out by Noah to establish whether the waters had receded. For slaves, a similar hope existed— that their bondage might be over.

At the request of Governor John Andrew of Massachusetts (panel 27), Harriet Tubman volunteered to serve the Union forces and was sent to Beaufort, South Carolina, on a government transport ship in May 1862. She worked for the Union Army for about three years. Initially she assisted the large numbers of newly freed blacks who had fled into the Union lines, where she helped the sick and destitute to survive and support themselves. Although paid no salary, she was allowed to draw rations as a soldier, but she gave up her privileges because she wanted to be a clear example of independence and self-sufficiency to the people she was helping. To support herself she made pies, gingerbread, and root beer in her off-hours and sold them. Harriet found herself in a strange situation: she had been asked to serve the government but she had to make her own way, receiving only an initial stipend of $200 to establish herself.[34]

Panel 27 portrays a black regiment moving boldly into the field. Reiterated angular running shapes set up a rhythm across the picture plane. A red flower springs in the lower right corner, recalling a similar symbol of hope in the *Frederick Douglass* series. Dark blue uniforms are edged in green on the sleeve edges; this free use of color is a device the artist also employs in the *Douglass* series.

Harriet was invaluable as an intelligence gatherer. She organized spy and scouting corps, and her intimate knowledge of the local terrain proved to be a major contribution to the guerrilla warfare utilized in the Southeastern war zones; she was also reputed to be an extraordinarily skilled guerrilla fighter. She served as an effective liaison in the South, understood by both Southern blacks and Union soldiers. From the slaves, she learned the positions of armies and batteries, and was known for "displaying remarkable courage, zeal, and fidelity."[35] In panel 28, Lawrence portrays Harriet Tubman talking with a group of slaves. He uses the Byzantine convention of depicting figures clustered like grapes to indicate spatial recession—a witty portrayal of Harriet gaining the confidence of the group. The familiar woven baskets and slave cabins are present; the artist's delight in invention is conveyed through Harriet's yellow shoes.

Harriet Tubman was also a hard-working nurse during the Civil War. She applied her skills with herbal medicine to curing maladies of the South. In panel 29, Harriet feels the pulse of an ailing soldier. The "disease" alluded to in the caption has been variously identified as dysentery, small pox, and malaria by Bradford and Conrad.[36] The two figures in the painting are assembled in a Pietà grouping, continuing the crucifixion and sacrificial themes underlying the works of the series. Compelling focus is created by the pyramidal pairing of the dark and light silhouettes. Harriet's strong presence is conveyed through scale. Her big hand expressively supports the soldier's head, and his figure seems frail before her ample form floating in the shadowless, textured picture plane. In the panels of the *Tubman* series, all soldiers depicted are black: Lawrence emphasizes the contribution of blacks to the cause of freedom.

The Civil War ended with the surrender of General Robert E. Lee at Appomattox on April 9 and of General Johnston at Greensboro on April 26, 1865. Panel 30 symbolically asserts the conclusion of the conflict.

Bayonets are thrust into the soil with a stiff finality, while the blood of the sacrifice they exacted seeps into the earth. Above them, the dove returns across the desolate, empty battleground. Shadows lie behind the weapons as if they were dramatically lit from the front, giving an unusual complexity and spatial dimension to this image.

After her war service, when Harriet Tubman returned home to Auburn, she found her house about to be sold to satisfy a mortgage foreclosure, and she lacked the means to redeem it. To aid her, abolitionist Sarah Bradford quickly wrote Tubman's biography, and all proceeds from the book went to Harriet. After the war, Harriet Tubman devoted her life to assisting blacks in distress.

In 1869, Harriet had married Nelson Davis, whom she had met in the South during the war. He had been a private in a black volunteer regiment. She tried unsuccessfully to obtain payment from the government for her wartime service, and supported herself through domestic work, growing and selling produce and poultry, and by donations.

She lived to attend the funeral of her friend the abolitionist Wendell Phillips in Boston in February 1883, which was also attended by Frederick Douglass; she also went to the funeral for Douglass, whose death was quite a blow to her. Harriet Tubman contributed to the Women's Suffrage movement and was friends with Susan B. Anthony and Elizabeth Cady Stanton. When she was almost eighty years old, the government gave her a pension of $20 per month, and she founded a home for the aged and indigent.

Harriet Tubman remained very active, and despite her old head injury, which plagued her with daily episodes of somnolence, she lived into her nineties.[37] She died on March 10, 1913, and was buried with military honors; her death was reported widely in the newspapers (an obituary appeared in *The New York Times*, March 14, 1913). The caption to panel 31 alludes

to the dedication ceremony at which a bronze com-
memorative tablet was placed on the Cayuga County
Courthouse in Auburn. The memorial ceremony was
held June 12, 1914, and was attended by thousands of
people.[38]

Panel 31 offers for a final time the dark sky, moon
and stars, and austere landscape through which Harriet passed on her many trips to rescue slaves. In a
letter Frederick Douglass wrote to Tubman, he refers
to the night sky and stars:

The difference between us is very marked. Most that I have
done and suffered in the service of our cause has been in
public, and I have received much encouragement at every
step of the way. You, on the other hand, have labored in a
private way. I have wrought in the day—you in the night. I
have had the applause of the crowd and the satisfaction that
comes of being approved by the multitude, while the most
that you have done has been witnessed by a few trembling,
scared, and foot-sore bondmen and women, whom you have
led out of the house of bondage, and whose heartfelt "God
bless you" has been your only reward. The midnight sky and
the silent stars have been the witnesses of your devotion to
freedom and of your heroism. Excepting John Brown—of
sacred memory—I know of no one who has willingly encountered more perils and hardships to serve our enslaved people
than you have. . . . [39]

Douglass's letter, included in the Bradford book, may
have been a source for Jacob Lawrence's emblematic
emphasis on the features of the night sky and stars in
the series.

THE *Harriet Tubman* series is delicate, elegant in style,
showing Jacob Lawrence's increasing facility with his
new medium, casein tempera. The graceful black
silhouettes in many panels are reminiscent of the time-
less figural simplicity of Greek black-figure vase painting and Egyptian murals.

In the *Tubman* series, Lawrence treats the protagonist as he did in the *Douglass* series: he focuses on

FIGURE 5 *Harriet Tubman, c. 1880. Photograph courtesy of
the Schomburg Center for Research in Black Culture, New York
Public Library.*

Harriet Tubman's unique contributions to the struggle
for freedom from slavery but does not offer a full
biography. Taking his cue from the available literature, especially the Bradford account, the artist has
presented Harriet Tubman as a strong, courageous,
tenacious person capable of enormous self-sacrifice.
He selects for portrayal those aspects of Tubman's per-
sonality and character that were monumental and inspiring, and sets them off against a backdrop of Old
Testament allusions and numerous compositional and
symbolic references to the sacrifice of Christ.

The artist's use of captions in the *Tubman* series differs slightly from the *Douglass* series. Because of the
unavailability of autobiographical material for Harriet
Tubman, the series' captions are based, in the main,
on Bradford's text and offer quotes from other material

as well. The artist attempts to convey Tubman's manner of expression, as reported in the literature, in her reputed prayers, songs, and exclamations (e.g., panels 13, 23, and 25). Lawrence also uses many examples of humor in the *Tubman* series, no doubt because Tubman was also known to be quite a prankster.[40] Lawrence alternates sober panels with light-hearted imagery, setting up an emotional rhythm in the sequence of paintings to relieve the pain and tension of the unfolding story.[41]

One major significance of the *Harriet Tubman* series is the artist's choice to deal with this important but little-known figure in the abolitionist struggle. Even very recent literature and reference sources exclude discussion of Harriet Tubman's role in the abolitionist movement; even so standard a reference as the *Encyclopedia Britannica* includes Frederick Douglass but not Harriet Tubman (both the regular and the young people's editions). There are only two major books about her, Bradford's and Conrad's—the latter not published until several years after Lawrence finished the series. Frederick Douglass, of course, produced his own history through his autobiographies and his other writings, whereas Harriet, being illiterate, was unable to record the events in her life. In addition, among those participating in the Underground Railroad, it was customary for self-protection not to keep any records—an attitude reinforced when John Brown's conviction was based in part on his confiscated papers. According to Bradford, Harriet Beecher Stowe had planned to write a book about Harriet Tubman, a project that never came to pass.[42]

Beyond these facts, the lack of historical material on Harriet Tubman is not only part of a long neglect of African-American history by mainstream American historians. It also may be related to a seemingly entrenched avoidance of active interest in the achievements of women in America, as well as the then-acceptable assumption that women could be expected to volunteer their services. The fact that she was a black woman further enforced her obscurity. This interpretation is confirmed by the government's treatment of Harriet Tubman regarding her Civil War service: while her husband received a war pension, she was not paid for her services and received no pension until about thirty years later, mainly owing to much effort by others on her behalf.

Strangely enough, Frederick Douglass excluded Tubman from his autobiographical accounts, even though they were friends and frequently colleagues in the Underground Railroad, and he may have set up her meeting with John Brown. Although Douglass's accounts are singularly egocentric, this omission is particularly curious when one considers the section in his later autobiography where he makes special mention of the "extraordinary efforts of women to the antislavery cause," and even here Tubman is not included.[43]

In his 1943 book, Conrad presents an analysis of Harriet Tubman's achievements by 1859, in an attempt to rectify this oversight:

. . . Her record in the 1850s alone . . . would have secured for her a lasting position among Americans as the ablest woman revolutionary, and a conspirator with but few peers among men. . . . For a half century the Underground system had been plunging its roots into the political fabric of the North and South. For the past ten years it had, like some huge social lever, separated the two sections, and rendered irreparable the breach. Millions of dollars worth of slaves, a total of 50,000, with an average value of $1,000 apiece, had flown to the North. Harriet had herself "stolen" about $300,000 worth of fellow blacks and stimulated other hundreds to flight. . . . Moreover, the uniform success of her campaigns was a record unrealized by any of the other conductors; and the excellence of her achievement lay in the fact that she was never martyred, never jailed, and never even for a day did she fall into the hands of her enemies, but outwitted them at every point.

. . . The moral influence [of Harriet Tubman's achievement] upon the Abolitionists, the economic consequences in weakening the slaveholders, the increased stimulus to Negro morale in the South, and the culminating political result in intensifying the North-South contradictions, still add up to the career of an unparalleled conspirator and social fighter in any clime, in any nation, in any period of history. Her leadership . . . created such a total effect in the ante-bellum period, laying siege, as it did, to the South's fundamental nature—the forceful containment of Negroes in slavery—that the prolonged guerrilla operation can only be called the Battle of the Underground, and it must be compared to the victorious command of a major front in the Civil War itself.[44]

Jacob Lawrence returned to the Harriet Tubman theme in 1968, when he illustrated a children's book, *Harriet and the Promised Land*. Allowed to choose a theme, he felt that Harriet's story would be especially suitable for children because "it is a dramatic tale of flight and fugitives."[45] The book reproduces seventeen gouache-on-paper paintings presented as full-page color reproductions accompanied by the story in verse. Although the two series based on Harriet Tubman's life are separated by almost thirty years, they share many similarities in stylistic and iconographical features.[46]

Because *Harriet and the Promised Land* was for children, many restrictions were placed on presentation of content. Nevertheless, when it was released, some reviewers considered the content of the book too visually disturbing for children. A New England librarian complained to Lawrence in a letter that the book made Harriet Tubman look grotesque and ugly, and Lawrence replied to her:

If you had walked in the fields, stopping for short periods to be replenished by Underground stations; if you couldn't feel secure until you reached the Canadian border, you too, madam, would look grotesque and ugly. Isn't it sad that the oppressed often find themselves grotesque and ugly and find the oppressor refined and beautiful?[47]

After the book was completed, censorship still rankling, Lawrence did a few more individual paintings on the Harriet Tubman theme just for himself without restrictions.[48] In 1973, the Brooklyn Museum and the Brooklyn Public Library awarded Lawrence the Books for Children citation for *Harriet and the Promised Land*.

The significance of the Harriet Tubman theme to Lawrence was revealed again in the late 1970s, when he was asked to paint a self-portrait for the National Academy of Design's collection. This 1977 work is Lawrence's only self-portrait, except for a few commissioned drawings. It shows Lawrence seated in his studio, surrounded by his art materials and several of his paintings. The paintings serve as symbols of his life and career; many are no longer in his possession. Over his shoulder most prominently hangs a work of the Harriet Tubman theme from 1968, a scene in which she guides fugitive slaves North.[49]

When I asked Jacob Lawrence why he had continued to pay so much artistic attention to Harriet Tubman through the years and not to Frederick Douglass, he said that Tubman's story had "more pictorial drama" than Frederick Douglass's. And, he added, " . . . because she's a woman. I don't think the black woman has been heralded or thought of—even less so than the black male."[50]

When the subjects are strong, I believe simplicity is the best way of treating them.

Jacob Lawrence, 1945

4
The Imagery of Struggle

THE *Frederick Douglass* and *Harriet Tubman* series are among five historical sequences that Jacob Lawrence painted consecutively during the first five years of his career (the other three are *Toussaint L'Ouverture,* 1937–38, *The Migration of the Negro,* 1940–41, and *John Brown,* 1941). All are concerned with the history of black Americans, their struggle against slavery, and their efforts to find freedom and a better life—themes with universal human resonance. In each series, the artist appended prose captions to each of the paintings.

The success of Lawrence's narrative series lies in the complementary power of image and caption, a union that comprises the artist's distinctive narrative conceptualization. The captions create a narrative fabric for the series. Caption material was chosen to emphasize those personal qualities of the heroes—such as courage, will—that were necessary for them to achieve their ends and visions.

In his captions, Lawrence also emphasizes the value of cooperating with all progressive factions of society, including whites—a value underlying not only Frederick Douglass's and Harriet Tubman's philosophies but also the artist's. Lawrence's captions tell the stories of these two persons factually, without rancor or propaganda. After opening both series with captions that deliver great emotional impact, he lets the stories and actions of the two heroes speak eloquently for themselves. While the content of each story is provocative, it is told and portrayed in a controlled manner. Lawrence, Douglass, and Tubman have much in common: their wisdom eliminates much anger.

These two series form a pair, stylistically and conceptually—a situation unique in Lawrence's body of work. They deal with the two mythic figures of the struggle against slavery in the United States, and their stories swell to a climax during the Civil War. Content is presented physically and conceptually in much the same manner. The paintings of these two series are of the same size; the series contain almost the same number of panels, and share a similar manner of presenting visual imagery complemented by biographical captions.[1] A primary aesthetic feature is their unity through the use of color, especially the umbers, greens, and blues.

Relying on invention and imagination, the artist offers compelling portrayals of another place and another era. Through his freeze-frame technique, the subject of the painting is made clear; the arrested movement of his figures, stopped in mid-stride or gesture, reads as decisive action. Focus is on heads, hands, and feet. Facial features are minimized: Lawrence, for the most part, is not concerned with individualism or portraiture. Simple concepts are rendered directly. Lawrence employs an intuitive expressionism, using distortion for emphasis.

As Lawrence tends to do in his work generally, desperate drama in these series is balanced by comic relief and light-hearted moments. As a sequence progresses, the artist alternates heavy with lighter content so that the viewer is not overwhelmed by each story's depressing aspects. Within his small format, Lawrence sustains a vigorous and exciting spatial dynamic through unusual perspectives, lively arrangement of color, exaggeration and abstraction of figural elements, and both repetition and variation of forms and motifs.

The two series also differ from each other in important ways. In content, the *Douglass* series is more narrative, more illustrative, while the *Tubman* series is more broadly philosophical, with more abstract and symbolic compositions. Both series are united by a common iconography: the barren brown landscape with clumps of mottled green vegetation, spiky, denuded trees, broad sky with streaming clouds, wide fearful eyes, sinister white slave owners, bayonets, chains, and the hopeful red flower. The *Douglass* series repeats the bare cabin interiors, and the *Tubman* series has vast open spaces in which human figures are diminished to convey isolation and alienation. Also repeated in the *Tubman* series are the snake, midnight sky with stars and moon, the sun, dove of peace, cotton plant, and the Pietà image.

Ultimately, the *Tubman* series is profoundly different from the *Douglass* series, in many contentual and formal aspects. With its emphasis on both Old Testament and New Testament iconography and allusive representations, the *Tubman* series is a substantial exploration on Lawrence's part of how to take leave of the literal pictorial narrative and approach the telling of a story on a symbolic level. Iconic compositions and allusions to exile and wilderness, the crucifixion, and the strong motif of sacrifice are evidence of an aesthetic and philosophical exploration to this point untried in Lawrence's oeuvre. Most of all, the *Harriet Tubman* series is a very personal expression for the artist—the first instance in which he combines so inventively in his art an accounting of history and his own private responses to it.

In style, most noticeable differences are in the artist's use of the medium. The *Douglass* series is darker in color: in most panels, the paint is laid on in opaque built-up layers, resulting in flat, unmodulated areas of color. By the time he painted the *Tubman* series, Lawrence had learned how to exploit the medium and explore texture with more painterly interest, applying paint thinly and allowing the gesso ground to show through, thus leaving more visible brushstrokes. Colors in the *Tubman* series are therefore often more subtly and expressively modulated. The sequence has more light and dark contrast, seen especially in the darker skin color of Harriet and the figures of the slaves. While both series show very little action of natural light, the artist uses stylized shaded areas on forms in the *Tubman* series, and in one panel (panel 30) he even indicates shadows extending from forms. Both series are in a dark palette, which is characteristic of the artist's work until the early 1940s.

Lawrence also achieved more variation in saturation of hue in the *Tubman* series. The biggest difference between it and the *Douglass* series is the blue of the sky. In the *Douglass* series, sky is always the same: pure blue with streaming white clouds or yellow moon. In the *Tubman* series, the artist differentiates day from night by sky color intensity: day is a cool grey-blue with a blue streaming cloud, and night is a deep cobalt blue, emphasizing the significance of Harriet's nocturnal journeys, with stars, moon, and light streaky clouds. Light to dark ranges of a particular color are achieved by increasing the layers of strokes of the same color. These painterly qualities enrich and vitalize the *Tubman* series.

Lawrence's approach to shape also differs in the two series: in the *Douglass* series forms are rounded, while in the *Tubman* series they are more linear, angular, with crisp silhouettes, and some are even delicately rendered. By the late 1930s, Lawrence was moving toward his strongly cubist-expressionist stylistic tendencies of the 1940s. In the *Harriet Tubman* series, compositions contain a more selective vocabulary of shapes, on the whole: bold forms are more prominent than in the *Douglass* series, and there are fewer subordinate details, as if Lawrence has become more concerned with symbolism and abstraction. On the other hand, drawing is emphasized: figural form is more articulated, elaborated, as if to counteract these stringent simplifications. *Harriet Tubman* has more arresting paintings, with forms more assured: panel 7, for example, is one of Lawrence's most powerful and engaging statements, and panels 2 and 9 present antislavery imagery with consummate genius and precision.

In the *Douglass* series, the artist often uses the exaggerated tilted perspective without horizon. The *Tubman* series employs deeper spatial recession, with a horizon line frequently evident. The vast, open landscapes of the *Tubman* series participate in elevating the themes of exile and sacrifice—strongly evoked by the references to biblical themes and iconography—to a universal rather than a particular landscape.

In emotional tone, the *Douglass* series, being more integrated with a historical narrative, is more straightforward, with some subtle irony and wit. In the *Tubman* series, Lawrence employs significantly more humor and variety of tone in general. The *Douglass* series illustrates mistreatment and portrays far more confrontational violence in which the protagonist interacts with others. In the *Tubman* series, violence is treated in a more symbolic, removed manner (e.g., panel 2). The artist has quickly acquired a more philosophical approach: one that implies rather than illustrates, one that presents allegorically rather than actually. This has become one of Lawrence's characteristic strengths: his ability to portray strident messages through subtle implication.

OVER THE more than fifty years of his career, Jacob Lawrence has maintained a consistent position as a figurative, narrative painter, for which he has earned much attention, both positive and negative, from critics. It can be asserted that Lawrence's greatest achievement as an artist lies in his series—in his ability to portray American historical narrative in vivid, authoritative compositional suites. In this strength, Lawrence offers a significant link in the traditions of American history painting, American Scene painting, and American figural art.

The *Frederick Douglass* and *Harriet Tubman* series, along with Lawrence's other early series, offer a didactic content unusual for this artist. In few other periods in his body of work is Lawrence's art so laden with overt messages; characteristically, it is more broadly philosophical.[2] The four early series on Toussaint, Douglass, Tubman, and Brown share this feature, indicating the artist's strong commitment to telling the meaningful sagas of these significant historical persons and rendering the stirring, incredible struggles they endured.

Much of the ultimate success of these works lies in the artist's own brand of soft-spoken protest, which can be understood through analysis of how his work attracts and holds the viewer's attention: Through compelling design and vibrant color, the viewer's attention is first attracted. The works are relatively small, requiring close scrutiny. When taking a close look, one then becomes aware of the wealth of intriguing human incident and supporting elements. Amusing revelations of human foibles and compassionate treatment of human figures lead to an involvement with the broader moral issues implied in the works: imagery is deeply touching; comic details delight. Like Giotto, Lawrence exhibits an intelligent wit, which he employs to enhance the accessibility and impact of his work.[3] Although the work depicts profound problems, one clings to the artist's optimism. The viewing public's typical resistance to powerful social commentary is overcome by Lawrence's ability to tell poignant human stories through colorful pattern, authoritative design, compelling narrative, beguiling figures and forms, and a balance of wit and power.

Lawrence has a strong sense of history and cultural continuity, as is evidenced not only in his American historical series but also in his individual paintings of genre scenes of social and political realities. He has a sensitive awareness of the interdependency of generations. As an example, in the 1960s, when rising black awareness was so vociferously expressed, Lawrence, because he was a teacher, was sometimes considered by students to be part of the Establishment. At that time, he said, he wanted to tell them, "Look, I've been through some things, too, and so have the people before my generation, and they're the ones who made it possible for you to have this kind of protest."[4] Lawrence had in mind, no doubt, the struggles of Douglass and Tubman, among others.

In one of Lawrence's recent single paintings, *Bread, Fish, and Fruit* (1986), the imagery draws from the entire body of his work. A carpenter's family sits around a table, heads bowed in prayer before a meal. Their home has an interior of rough-cut umber boards resembling the slaves' quarters in the *Frederick Douglass* series of almost fifty years before. Lawrence has revived this symbolic environment as a regenerative act, showing the continuity of his themes and his commitment to heritage.

Jacob Lawrence still respects the paintings of the *Frederick Douglass* and *Harriet Tubman* series after these many decades. In April 1988, he had the opportunity to view them all together again, and in a lecture at the Hirshhorn Museum he remarked: "They are some of the most successful statements I have made in my life. I couldn't repeat them now."[5]

THE *Frederick Douglass* and *Harriet Tubman* series are among Jacob Lawrence's greatest achievements as a painter. At times powerfully exquisite, at other times raw, even awkward, their rough magic and expressive strength speak to us through time of the often-neglected episodes of black American history and the black experience. Lawrence has explained:

If at times my productions do not express the conventionally beautiful, there is always an effort to express the universal beauty of man's continuous struggle to lift his social position and to add dimension to his spiritual being.[6]

Paintings and Captions

FIGURE 6 *Jacob Lawrence teaching, 1984. Photo by Chris Eden.*

NOTE: For further information on historical issues and persons mentioned in the paintings' captions as well as for further elaboration on the paintings' content, see the notes to Chapters 2 and 3 of the text. The paintings for the *Frederick Douglass* and *Harriet Tubman* series are reproduced here in their intended sequence and with their captions. All paintings are casein tempera on gessoed hardboard, 12 by 17⅞ inches in dimension. The paintings are owned by the Hampton University Museum, Hampton, Virginia. Photographs are by Scott Wolff.

Frederick Douglass (1938–39)

I. THE SLAVE

1. In Talbot County, eastern shore, state of Maryland,
in a thinly populated worn-out district inhabited by a
white population of the lowest order, among slaves who
in point of ignorance were fully in accord with their
surroundings—it was here that Frederick Douglass was
born and spent the first years of his childhood—
February 1818.

2. One of the barbarous laws of the slave system was
that of hiring out members of families who were slaves,
this occurring in the Douglass family. The only recollec-
tions he had of his mother were those few hasty visits
she made to him during the night.

3. When old enough to work, he was taken to Colonel Lloyd's slave master. His first introduction to the realities of the slave system was the flogging of Millie, a slave on the Lloyd plantation.

4. In the slaves' living quarters, the children slept in
holes and corners of the huge fireplaces. Old and
young, married and single, slept on clay floors.

5. The master's quarters or "the great house" was filled with luxuries. It possessed the finest of foods from Europe, Asia, Africa, and the Caribbean. It contained fifteen servants. It was one of the finest mansions in the South.

6. Hired out from Colonel Lloyd's plantation, Frederick Douglass arrived in Baltimore at the age of eight. His new mistress, never before having been a slaveholder, consented to his request to teach him to read, to which the master of the house told her the laws of the slave system—one being that a slave must only learn one thing—to obey—1826.

7. Douglass, forced by his master to discontinue his learning, continued his studies with his white friends who were in school.

8. Frederick Douglass, having earned a few cents as a bootblack, purchased *The Columbian Orator*. In this book he studied Sheridan's speeches on the Catholic Emancipation, Lord Chatham's speech on the American war, and speeches by the great William Pitt and Fox.

9. Transferred back to the eastern shore of Maryland,
being one of the few Negroes who could read or write,
Douglass was approached by James Mitchell, a free
Negro, and asked to help teach a Sabbath school. However, their work was stopped by a mob who threatened
them with death if they continued their class—1833.

10. The master of Douglass, seeing he was of a rebellious nature, sent him to a Mr. Covey, a man who had built up a reputation as a "slave breaker." A second attempt by Covey to flog Douglass was unsuccessful. This was one of the most important incidents in the life of Frederick Douglass: he was never attacked again by Covey. His philosophy: a slave easily flogged is flogged oftener; a slave who resists flogging is flogged less.

11. The slaves were invariably given a Christmas and New Year's holiday, which they spent in various ways, such as hunting, ball playing, boxing, foot racing, dancing, and drinking— the latter being encouraged the most by the slaveholders, this being the most effective way of keeping down the spirit of insurrection among slaves.

12. It was in 1836 that Douglass conceived a plan of escape, also influencing several slaves around him. He told his co-conspirators what had been done, dared, and suffered by men to obtain the inestimable boon of liberty.

13. As the time of their intended escape drew nearer, their anxiety grew more and more intense. Their food was prepared and their clothing packed. Douglass had forged their passes. Early in the morning they went into the fields to work. At mid-day they were all called off the field, only to discover that they had been betrayed.

14. Frederick Douglass was sent to Baltimore to work in the shipyards of Gardiner. Here the workers were Negro slaves and a poor class of whites. The slaveholders caused much friction between the two groups. It was in one of the many brawls here that Douglass almost lost an eye. Douglass had become a master of his trade, that of ship caulker. Seeing no reason why at the end of each week he should give his complete earnings to a man he owed nothing, again he planned to escape.

II. THE FUGITIVE

15. Frederick Douglass's escape from slavery was a hazardous and exciting twenty-four hours. Douglass disguised himself as a sailor—best, he thought, because he knew the language of a sailor and he knew a ship from stem to stern. On he traveled through Maryland, Wilmington, Philadelphia, and to his destination, New York. Frederick Douglass was free.

16. Douglass's first three years in the North were spent as a laborer, on the wharfs, sawing wood, shoveling coal, digging cellars, and removing rubbish.

17. Douglass listened to lectures by William Lloyd Garrison. He heard him denounce the slave system in words that were mighty in truth and mighty in earnestness.

18. It was in the year 1841 that Frederick Douglass
joined the forces of William Lloyd Garrison and the
abolitionists. He helped secure subscribers to *The Anti-
Slavery Standard* and *The Liberator*. He lectured through
the eastern counties of Massachusetts, narrating his life
as a slave, telling of the cruelty, the inhuman and clan-
nish nature of the slave system.

19. The Garrisonians in the year 1843 planned a series
of conventions in order to spread and create greater
antislavery sentiment in New Hampshire, Vermont,
New York, Ohio, Indiana, and Pennsylvania. In one of
these conventions, Douglass and two of his fellow
workers were mobbed at Pendleton, Indiana.

20. Frederick Douglass left America to lecture in Great Britain. Here he met some of the most progressive and liberal-minded men in the English-speaking world. He made a great speech in Covent Garden Theatre on August 7, 1846, in which he told of the people he represented—how at that moment there were three million colored slaves in the United States.

21. Leaving England in the spring of 1847 with a large sum of money given him by sympathizers of the antislavery movement, he arrived in Rochester, New York, and founded the Negro paper *The North Star*. As editor of *The North Star*, he wrote of the many current topics affecting the Negro, such as the Free Soil Convention at Buffalo, the nomination of Martin Van Buren, the Fugitive Slave Law, and the Dred Scott Decision.

22. Another important branch of Frederick Douglass's antislavery work was the Underground Railroad, of which he was the stationmaster for Rochester, controlling Lake Ontario and the Queen's Dominions.

23. It was in 1847 at Springfield, Massachusetts, that Frederick Douglass first met Captain John Brown, one of the strongest fighters for the abolishment of slavery. Here, John Brown talked with Douglass about his plan to fight slavery. He had been long looking for a man such as Douglass, as an admirer and champion of Negro rights—he had found the man.

24. John Brown discussed with Frederick Douglass his plan to attack Harper's Ferry, an arsenal of the United States Government. Brown's idea was to attack the arsenal and seize the guns. Douglass argued against this plan, his reason being that the abolishment of slavery should not occur through revolution.

NOTE: Discrepancies between the panel numbers on the corners of the paintings and the numbers given in the captions are explained on page 13, "Introduction," and on pages 114–15, note 20 to Chapter 2.

25. With Abraham Lincoln of the Republican party
elected president of the United States, with states
threatening their withdrawal from the Union—thus the
country in war fever—the abolitionists made their
speeches frequently and were more often attacked by
those who relished slavery.

26. The North and South were at war. Governor Andrew of Massachusetts asked the help of Frederick Douglass in securing two colored regiments. Douglass spoke before the colored men of Massachusetts. He told them that a war fought for the perpetual enslavement of the colored people called logically and loudly for colored men to help suppress it. He brought to their memories Denmark Vesey and Nat Turner, and Shields Green and John Copeland who fought side by side with John Brown. The 54th and 55th colored regiments were mustered.

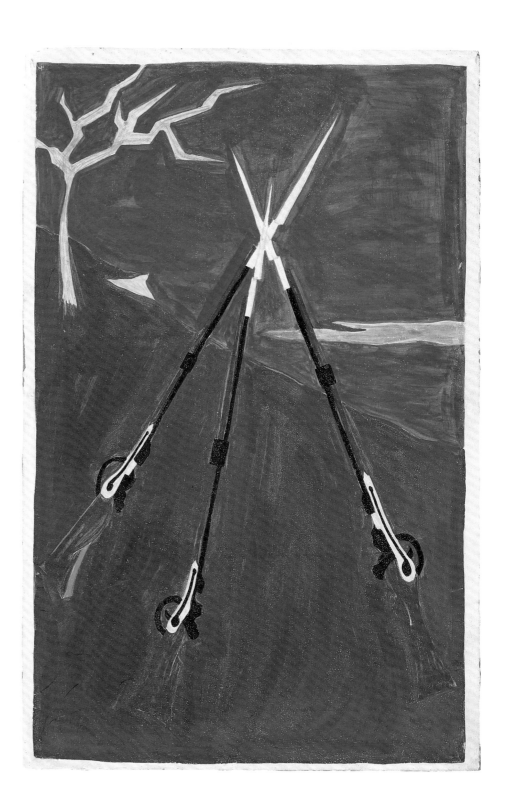

27. The government, having assured colored men that if they went into the battlefield their treatment would be the same as for whites, and not keeping its promise, Douglass protested, and his protest led him to Washington and to President Lincoln. Lincoln, proving to be a man of great human qualities, gave Frederick Douglass confidence and encouragement. Douglass left with the feeling that the black man's salvation was on the battlefield.

28. A cowardly and bloody riot took place in New York in July 1863—a mob fighting the draft, a mob willing to fight to free the Union, a mob unwilling to fight to free slaves, a mob that attacked every colored person within reach disregarding sex or age. They hanged Negroes, burned their homes, dashed out the brains of young children against the lamp posts. The colored populace took refuge in cellars and garrets. This mob was a part of the rebel force, without the rebel uniform but with all its deadly hate. It was the fire of the enemy opened in the rear of the loyal army.

III. The Free Man

29. The war was over. The slaves were literally turned out by their masters into a world unknown to them. They had ceased to be the slaves of man and had become the slaves of nature.

30. An appointment to any important and lucrative office under the United States Government usually brings its recipient a large measure of praise and congratulations on the one hand and much abuse and disparagement on the other. With these two conditions prevailing, Frederick Douglass was appointed by President Rutherford B. Hayes to be United States marshal of the District of Columbia, 1877.

31. During the exodus, thousands of poor Negroes left
the South in search of better country. Douglass spoke
of this movement at the Social Science Congress at
Saratoga, New York. "The habit of roaming from place
to place is never a good one until a man has endeavored
to make his immediate surroundings in accord with his
wishes. The business of this government is to protect
its citizens where they are, and not send them where
they do not need protection."

32. Frederick Douglass revisited the eastern shore of Maryland—here he was born a slave, now he returned a free man. He left unknown to the outside world and returned well known. He left on a freight boat and returned on a United States revenue cutter. He was a citizen of the United States of America.

Harriet Tubman (1939–40)

1. "With sweat and toil and ignorance he consumes his life, to pour the earnings into channels from which he does not drink." ——Henry Ward Beecher

2. "I am no friend of slavery, but I prefer the liberty of my own country to that of another people, and the liberty of my own race to that of another race. The liberty of the descendants of Africa in the United States is incompatible with the safety and liberty of the European descendants. Their slavery forms an exception (resulting from a stern and inexorable necessity) to the general liberty in the United States." ——Henry Clay

3. "A house divided against itself cannot stand. I believe that this government cannot last permanently half slave and half free. I do not expect this union to be dissolved; I do not expect the house to fall, but I do expect it will cease to be divided. It will become all one thing or the other."
——Abraham Lincoln

4. On a hot summer day about 1820, a group of slave children were tumbling in the sandy soil in the state of Maryland—and among them was one, Harriet Tubman. Dorchester County, Maryland.

5. She felt the first sting of slavery when as a young girl she was struck on the head with an iron bar by an enraged overseer.

6. Harriet heard the shrieks and cries of women who were being flogged in the Negro quarter. She listened to their groaned-out prayer, "Oh Lord, have mercy."

7. Harriet Tubman worked as water girl to field hands. She also worked at plowing, carting, and hauling logs.

8. Whipped and half starved to death, Harriet Tubman's
skull injury often caused her to fall faint while at work.
Her master, not having any more use for her, auctioned
her off to the highest bidder.

9. Harriet Tubman dreamt of freedom ("Arise! Flee for your life!"), and in the visions of the night she saw the horsemen coming. Beckoning hands were ever motioning her to come, and she seemed to see a line dividing the land of slavery from the land of freedom.

10. Harriet Tubman was between twenty and twenty-five years of age at the time of her escape. She was now alone. She turned her face toward the North, and fixing her eyes on the guiding star, she started on her long, lonely journey.

11. "$500 Reward! Runaway from subscriber on Thursday night, the 4th inst., from the neighborhood of Cambridge, my negro girl, Harriet, sometimes called Minty. Is dark chestnut color, rather stout build, but bright and handsome. Speaks rather deep and has a scar over the left temple. She wore a brown plaid shawl.

I will give the above reward captured outside the county, and $300 if captured inside the county, in either case to be lodged in the Cambridge, Maryland, jail.

(Signed) George Carter
Broadacres, near Cambridge, Maryland,
September 24th, 1849"

12. Night after night, Harriet Tubman traveled, occasionally stopping to buy bread. She crouched behind trees or lay concealed in swamps by day until she reached the North.

13. "I had crossed the line of which I had been dreaming. I was free, but there was no one to welcome me to the land of freedom. Come to my help, Lord, for I am in trouble."

14. Seeking help, Harriet Tubman met a lady who ushered her to a haycock, and Harriet found herself in a strange room, round and tapering to a peak. Here she rested and was fed well, and she continued on her way. It was Harriet Tubman's first experience with the Underground Railroad.

15. In the North, Harriet Tubman worked hard. All her wages she laid away for the one purpose of liberating her people, and as soon as a sufficient amount was secured she disappeared from her Northern home, and as mysteriously appeared one dark night at the door of one of the cabins on the plantation, where a group of trembling fugitives was waiting. Then she piloted them North, traveling by night, hiding by day, scaling the mountains, wading the rivers, threading the forests— she, carrying the babies, drugged with paragoric. So she went, nineteen times liberating over 300 pieces of living, breathing "property."

16. Harriet Tubman spent many hours at the office of
William Still, the loft headquarters of the antislavery
Vigilance Committee in Philadelphia. Here, she pored
over maps and discussed plans with the keen, educated
young secretary of that mysterious organization, the
Underground Railroad, whose main branches stretched
like a great network from the Mississippi River to
the coast.

17. Like a half-crazed sybilline creature, she began to haunt the slave masters, stealing down in the night to lead a stricken people to freedom.

18. At one time during Harriet Tubman's expeditions into the South, the pursuit after her was very close and vigorous. The woods were scoured in all directions, and every person was stopped and asked: "Have you seen Harriet Tubman?"

19. Such a terror did she become to the slaveholders that a reward of $40,000 was offered for her head, she was so bold, daring, and elusive.

20. In 1850, the Fugitive Slave Law was passed, which bound the people north of the Mason and Dixon Line to return to bondage any fugitives found in their territories—forcing Harriet Tubman to lead her escaped slaves into Canada.

21. Every antislavery convention held within 500 miles of Harriet Tubman found her at the meeting. She spoke in words that brought tears to the eyes and sorrow to the hearts of all who heard her speak of the suffering of her people.

22. Harriet Tubman, after a very trying trip North in which she had hidden her cargo by day and had traveled by boat, wagon, and foot at night, reached Wilmington, where she met Thomas Garrett, a Quaker who operated an Underground Railroad station. Here, she and the fugitives were fed and clothed and sent on their way.

23. "The hounds are baying on my track,
    Old master comes behind,
    Resolved that he will bring me back,
    Before I cross the line."

24. It was the year 1859, five years after Harriet
Tubman's first trip to Boston. By this time, there was
hardly an antislavery worker who did not know the
name Harriet Tubman. She had spoken in a dozen
cities. People from here and abroad filled her hand
with money. And over and over again, she made her
mysterious raids across the border into the South.

25. Harriet Tubman was one of John Brown's friends. John Brown and Frederick Douglass crossed into Canada and arrived at the town of St. Catharines, a settlement of fugitive slaves, former "freight" of the Underground Railroad. Here, Douglass had arranged for a meeting with "Moses." She was Harriet Tubman: huge, deepest ebony, muscled as a giant, with a small close-curled head and anguished eyes—this was the woman John Brown came to for help. "I will help," she said.

26. In 1861, the first gun was fired on Fort Sumter, and the war of the Rebellion was on.

27. Governor John Andrew of Massachusetts, knowing
well the brave, sagacious character of Harriet Tubman,
sent for her and asked her if she could go at a moment's
notice to act as a spy and scout for the Union Army and,
if need be, to act as a hospital nurse. In short, to be
ready for any required service for the Union cause.

28. Harriet Tubman went into the South and gained the confidence of the slaves by her cheerful words and sacred hymns. She obtained from them valuable information.

29. She nursed the Union soldiers and knew how, when
they were dying by large numbers of some malignant
disease, with cunning skill to extract a healing draught
from roots and herbs that grew near the source of the
disease, thus allaying the fever and restoring soldiers
to health.

30. The war was over, men were being mustered out,
and regiments melted away overnight. For Lincoln's
words were now not paper words: they had been
written in the travail and blood of the men whom
Harriet Tubman had known.

31. Harriet Tubman spent the rest of her life in Auburn, New York. When she died, a large mass meeting was held in her honor. And on the outside of the county courthouse, a memorial tablet of bronze was erected.

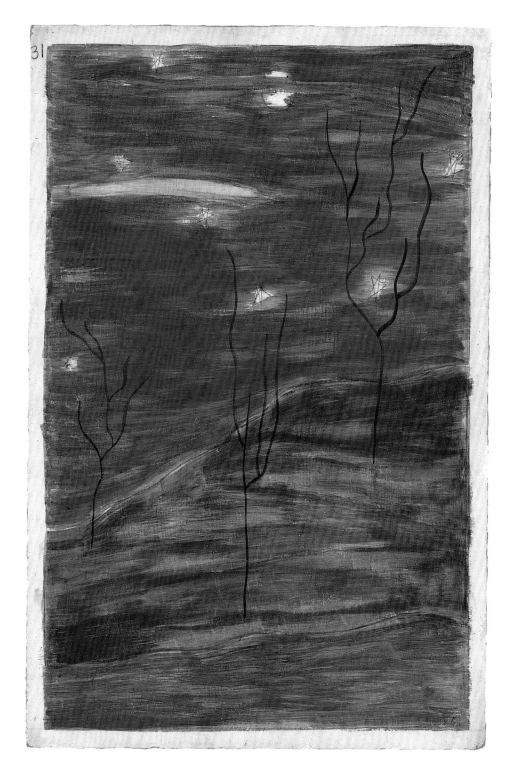

Notes

Introduction (pp. 12–13)

1 The two series were shown together for the first time since 1940 in 1978 at the Detroit Institute of Arts, as an adjunct to a show focusing on Lawrence's *John Brown* series owned by the Institute. They were shown at The Hampton University Museum in early 1989.

2 Jacob Lawrence had given the *Frederick Douglass* and *Harriet Tubman* series to the Harmon Foundation separately in 1939 and 1940 as he completed them, receiving a loan of about $100 for each and offering the paintings as collateral on the loans. He never paid back the loans and never took back the paintings. The series remained in the possession of the Harmon Foundation until the organization disbanded in 1967 and donated its art collection to various universities (e.g., Hampton University, Fisk University).

3 John R. McKivigan, managing editor of the Frederick Douglass Papers Project at Yale University, has pointed out to me that their project generally states that there are not four but three Douglass autobiographies, with the final one (1881) being substantially revised and enlarged in 1892.

1
Jacob Lawrence and the Series Format (pp. 15–17)

The epigraph for this chapter is from a statement Jacob Lawrence made early in his career. Revealing his motivation to interpret black history through a series of paintings, he was describing the *Toussaint L'Ouverture* series project a few years after completing it and just after he had finished the *Douglass* and *Tubman* series. Harmon Foundation, Jacob Lawrence Biographical Sketch (November 12, 1940), Downtown Gallery Papers, Microfilm Roll ND5 (55/590), Archives of American Art, Smithsonian Institution, Washington, D.C. The *Toussaint L'Ouverture* series is part of The Amistad Research Center's Aaron Douglas Collection, New Orleans. Lawrence's quote from Frederick Douglass is based on his recollection and is not a completely accurate quotation.

1 For details on Lawrence's life and work, see Ellen Harkins Wheat, *Jacob Lawrence, American Painter* (Seattle: University of Washington Press, 1986).

2 The impact of the Harlem Renaissance on the young Lawrence is discussed at length in Wheat, *Jacob Lawrence, American Painter*, pp. 26 ff. Bibliography on the era is also provided therein, p. 193, note 3.

3 For a discussion of the "306" studio, see Wheat, *Jacob Lawrence, American Painter*, pp. 29 ff.

4 While other modernist painters have employed the serial format (e.g., Robert Motherwell, Barnett Newman), their series have generally been formal explorations of a theme and executed over time, as opposed to Lawrence's use of the series as an opportunity to present narrative content in sequential units. Ben Shahn's use of the series format most closely resembles Lawrence's, but Lawrence disavows any awareness of Shahn's work before the early 1940s. See Wheat, *Jacob Lawrence, American Painter*, p. 42, for further discussion of this issue.

5 The Schomburg Collection is the largest accumulation of African-American studies materials in the world. The collection, which is part of the New York Public Library system, is now called the Schomburg Center for Research in Black Culture.

6 Jacob Lawrence, in conversation with the author, February 3 and 4, 1984.

7 Concerning the numbering of the *Frederick Douglass* series, see "Introduction," above.

8 Jacob Lawrence, in conversation with the author, February 3, 1984.

2
The *Frederick Douglass* Series (pp. 19–29)

Notes for the *Frederick Douglass* and *Harriet Tubman* series include explanations of issues and persons alluded to in the captions to the paintings, as well as further interpretations of the paintings' content.

Valuable sources for biographical information on Frederick Douglass were the four versions of Douglass's autobiography: *Narrative of the Life of Frederick Douglass, an American Slave, Written by Himself* (1845), and edited by Benjamin Quarles, 1960; *My Bondage and My Freedom* (1855), 1968; *Life and Times of Frederick Douglass, Written by Himself* (1881), 1983 facsimile edition with original introduction by George L. Ruffin; and *Life and Times of Frederick Douglass, Written by Himself* (1892), with an introduction by Rayford W. Logan, Howard University, 1962, and a useful index. The notes refer to the four versions by date, e.g., Douglass, 1845, Douglass, 1881, etc. Four other major sources were Benjamin Quarles, *Frederick Douglass*, 1970, a reprint of the 1948 edition; Philip Foner, *The Life and Writings of Frederick Douglass*, 1950–75, Vols. I–V, writings from 1841–61; Dickson J. Preston, *Young Frederick Douglass: The Maryland Years*, 1980; and John W. Blassingame, *The Frederick Douglass Papers*, Vol. I, 1985.

The epigraph for this chapter is from Foner, *Life and Writings*, Vol. I, p. 11.

1 There is evidence to support Frederick Douglass's having been born in either 1817 or 1818 (see Douglass, 1881, pp. 14, 449; Nathan Irvin Huggins, *Slave and Citizen: The Life of Frederick Douglass*, 1980, p. 181; and Dickson J. Preston, *Young Frederick Douglass: The Maryland Years*, 1980, pp. 9, 31 ff.). Frederick Douglass was born on a Maryland plantation owned by a Colonel Edward Lloyd. His birthdate is unrecorded, which is the case for most slaves, but he believed it to be February 1817 because of a remark he overheard made by his master. (For a full discussion of this issue, see Preston, pp. 31 ff.) Colonel Lloyd's chief agent, the slave master, was Captain Aaron Anthony. Douglass's father was white and his mother was of African heritage; it was rumored that Douglass's master was his father (Douglass's account does not make it clear to me whether he means Lloyd or Anthony). Douglass presumed that Captain Anthony received his title through having sailed a ship on Chesapeake Bay (Douglass, 1845, pp. 23–27).

2 Quoted in Douglass, 1845, in the introduction by Benjamin Quarles, p. viii; Quarles gives no source for this quote.

3 Quarles, in Douglass, 1845, pp. xiii ff., discusses the importance of Douglass's first version of his autobiography as a powerful tool in the abolition movement.

The Constitution of the United States (1787) included a provision known as the "rendition clause." Applying to indentured servants and apprentices and interpreted to extend to slaves, it read: "No person held to service or labour in one state, under the laws thereof, escaping into another, shall, in consequence of any law or regulation therein, be discharged from such service or labour, but shall be delivered up on claim of the party to whom such service or labour be due" (Art. IV, Sec. II, Par. 3).

The Fugitive Slave Act was passed in 1793 to provide for the return of slaves who escaped from one state into another state or territory. Both free blacks and manumitted slaves had to carry freedom papers attesting their civil status, and escaped slaves were constantly sought by owners or their agents. Under the act, a $500 fine was imposed on anyone who helped a slave escape or hid him or her from his or her master. Northern state officials were responsible for enforcing the law.

The act aroused much sympathy for runaway slaves; in 1794, abolitionist activity developed and an "Underground Railroad" began to be formed. In 1850, the Fugitive Slave Law was passed to respond to the South's demand for more effective federal legislation regarding runaway slaves. Under that law, the fine for assisting slaves was $1,000 additional damages if the owner brought suit. The 1850 law was repealed in June 1864. See Quarles, *Black Abolitionists*, pp. 143–44, 154; and Jane H. and William H. Pease, *The Fugitive Slave Law and Anthony Burns: A Problem of Law Enforcement*, 1975. An important comprehensive source for the contribution of American blacks to the abolition movement in the United States is the volumes published by The Black Abolitionist Papers Project, C. Peter Ripley, editor, The Florida State University.

4 Douglass traveled in England, Ireland, Scotland, and Wales, where he met prominent abolitionists such as Thomas Clarkson. Douglass was heartened by the power and effectiveness of the English abolitionist movement. The Reform Movement (1769–1832) was an active force in England for parliamentary electoral reform, culminating in the English Reform Act of 1832. From the 1760s on, the Reform Movement included a strong faction working to abolish the slave trade. English antislavery agitators included Thomas Clarkson, Granville Sharpe, and William Wilberforce. Parliamentary discussions of abolition were introduced in 1788, and in 1807 a bill was passed abolishing the slave trade. In 1823, the Antislavery Society was formed, led by Clarkson and Wilberforce. In 1833, an Emancipation Bill was passed. See T. Elmes, *Thomas Clarkson*, 1854; T. Clarkson, *History of the Rise, Progress, and Accomplishment of the Abolition of African Slave Trade by the British Parliament*, 1808; the Wilberforce sons, *Life*, 1838, and *Correspondence*, 1840, of William Wilberforce; and R. Coupland, *The British Antislavery Movement*, 1933.

The North Star is discussed below, note 31.

5 Quarles in Douglass, 1845, p. xii. Frederick Douglass died on February 20, 1895, at Cedar Hill, his home. Funeral services were held on February 25 in Washington, D.C., and on February 26 in Rochester, New York. He was buried in Mount Hope Cemetery, Rochester.

6 Douglass, 1881, p. 487, describes his "several lives: slavery,

fugitive, comparative freedom, conflict and battle, and victory." Lawrence was no doubt influenced by these divisions in choosing the structure and section designations of his *Frederick Douglass* series. The 1881 Douglass text is divided into two untitled parts that represent his years as a slave and his years as a free man. The 1892 version is in three untitled parts, the first two covering the same periods and the third dealing with his later life.

7 Lawrence had previously used poster color on paper. He had learned about casein tempera from his friend, the artist Romare Bearden, in about 1937 (Carroll Greene, Jr., "Interview of Jacob Lawrence," Washington, D.C., Archives of American Art, Smithsonian Institution, October 25, 1968, p. 79). The *Frederick Douglass* series is Lawrence's first series of panel paintings on hardboard (masonite).

8 Douglass recalled seeing his mother only four or five times. He later learned that she had died when he was about seven years old (Douglass, 1845, pp. 24–25).

Douglass's 1881 account contains several illustrations of the story, including one of a night visit from his mother. A few of Lawrence's *Frederick Douglass* paintings appear to be remotely related to these drawings.

9 Jacob Lawrence, lecture, School of Art, University of Washington, Seattle, November 15, 1982.

10 Lawrence has said that he needs a certain amount of dramatic action in a story to be inspired to render it artistically; for example, he has remarked that he was not able to do a series on Sojourner Truth for that reason.

11 Douglass lived at the Anthony house until he was eight, in the charge of a woman who treated him harshly; he remembers always being cold and hungry. The woman about to be punished in panel 3 may have been a cousin of Douglass's named Millie (Douglass, 1845, pp. 27–29; Douglass, 1881, pp. 35–36). There is some confusion between the two autobiographical accounts regarding the identity of the first flogged female in his experience: Douglass, 1845, talks of Aunt Hester, but Douglass, 1881, mentions the "cousin from Tuckahoe."

12 In his autobiography, Douglass verbally makes the same contrast of poverty and luxury in circumstances and quarters between slaves and masters. See Douglass, 1881, Chapters VI and VII. Colonel Edward Lloyd's mansion was called Wye House.

13 Douglass worked in the Auld household in Baltimore for seven years (Douglass, 1845, Chronology, p. xxv; Douglass, 1881, pp. 69–74).

14 Douglass, 1881, pp. 69–70, explains that he asked Mrs. Auld to teach him to read, and that she consented, teaching him the alphabet and words of three or four letters before she was admonished by her husband to stop. Douglass goes on to name the friends to whom he felt indebted for spelling lessons (p. 74). The caption for panel 8 mentions *The Columbian Orator*, a very popular schoolbook that cost fifty cents (pp. 75–78). He bought it when he was about twelve years old (Douglass, 1845, pp. 67–68).

Also mentioned in the panel 8 caption are Richard B. Sheridan, Lord Chatham (William Pitt, Earl of Chatham), Charles James Fox, and William Pitt (second son of Lord Chatham), eighteenth century English statesmen who were inspirational orators. The "American War" was the American Revolutionary War.

15 Douglass, 1845, pp. 66–68, and Douglass, 1881, pp. 76–78.

16 In St. Michaels, Mr. Wilson was the only white man in the community who believed in instructing blacks. He asked Douglass to teach the Sabbath school; sessions were held at the house of a free black man named James Mitchell. Thomas Auld was part of the mob that ended the Sabbath school and threatened Douglass with being shot like Nat Turner (Douglass, 1881, p. 105).

17 Douglass remained at Covey's place for a year (1834), and he allots many pages of his autobiography to describing this dismal period in his life (Douglass, 1881, pp. 122–41). The fateful fight lasted for several hours (Douglass, 1845, pp. 94–95).

18 Panel 11: Douglass, 1881, pp. 143–46, discusses the cunning coercion and irony involved: how holiday pleasures were encouraged, to keep the slaves from reflecting on their condition. He points out that slaveholders encouraged degrading behavior, such as drunkenness, so that the slaves would return to their labors willingly, disgusted with themselves and what they had done with their "free time."

19 Douglass, 1881, pp. 154 and 158. The three betrayed slaves (panel 13) were taken to jail in Easton in 1836 (Douglass, 1881, p. 168).

20 At this point in the *Frederick Douglass* series, the panel numbered 14–15 had two numbered captions pasted on the back; the painting has long been identified as "panel 14–15" with a dual caption. Caption 14 refers to a brawl and caption 15 refers to Douglass being a ship caulker. The series arrived in this state at Hampton University in 1967. The paintings, according to my inspection, have penciled numbers on the front upper left corners in the artist's hand. Painting 14–15 contained the original number 14 in the corner, and the next painting, numbered 15, had its original number crossed out in red (in someone else's

hand) and changed to 16. Original painting 16 is then changed to 17, and so on up through painting 24; from then on the original numbering scheme is retained. The artist cannot recall the circumstances of the confusion.

I suspect that when the Harmon Foundation came into possession of the paintings from Lawrence soon after they were produced, it may have seemed unclear which captions went with which paintings at this point in the *Douglass* sequence because the numbered captions did not match the numbered images. It was probably the Harmon Foundation that changed the numbers in red and typed the caption labels pasted on the backs of the paintings. (It is not clear who typed the labels, but I know that they were affixed to the backs of the paintings by someone other than the artist, because the same red pencil that crossed out the numbers was also used to lay out ruled rectangles to position the labels—a finicky approach Lawrence would not use.) The artist does not believe that there is a missing painting; but the confused numbers remain a mystery. The Harmon Foundation papers in the Library of Congress are not enlightening on the two series in general.

I have worked with Jacob Lawrence to provide the series with a proper numbering sequence. The paintings are now numbered and captioned in accordance with the artist's wishes: panel 14 has a long caption representing the old dual caption 14–15, painting 15 is the former (later numbered) panel 16, and so on. The series now ends with panel 32, and the question of a supernumerary panel 33 has been resolved.

Douglass's tenure at Gardiner's shipyard (panel 14) is discussed in Douglass, 1881, pp. 176–87. The brawl scene alluded to in caption 14 is discussed in Douglass, 1881, pp. 182–83.

21 Douglass, 1881, p. 187.

22 In Douglass's 1845 autobiography, he withholds information regarding the manner of his escape in September 1838 because it might have prevented other slaves from using that means, and it might also have jeopardized the people who assisted him, and their property (Douglass, 1881, p. 196). In the 1881 autobiography, no longer needing to be cautious, he gives the details (see panel 15 caption). At many points during his escape journey, Douglass thought capture was imminent, especially because the description on the borrowed papers did not match his appearance closely, and papers of traveling blacks were always checked (Douglass, 1881, pp. 196 ff.).

23 In all versions of his autobiography (e.g., Douglass, 1892,

pp. 204–05), Douglass only mentions his first wife and children a few times in passing. In the 1892 work, he gives considerably more text space to his second wife (pp. 534 ff.).

24 Douglass, 1845, p. 152; and Douglass, 1881, p. 212.

25 Douglass, 1881, pp. 214–15. For a discussion of William Lloyd Garrison's impact on Douglass's life, see Quarles, *Black Abolitionists*, pp. 18–22. *The Liberator* was founded in January 1831 (see Filler, *The Crusade Against Slavery: 1830–1860*, 1960, p. 60; Quarles, *Black Abolitionists*, pp. 18–22.) *The Anti-Slavery Standard*, another major abolitionist journal, is discussed by Quarles, *Black Abolitionists*, p. 26.

26 Quarles in Douglass, 1845, p. viii.

27 Douglass, 1881, pp. 233–35.

28 Douglass, 1881, pp. 219–20, 236 ff.; see also note 3 above.

29 Douglass, 1881, pp. 250 ff., discusses his Covent Garden speech.

30 Ironically, some of Douglass's uncompromising abolitionist friends in New England objected to anyone's paying the ransom for Douglass's freedom from slavery. As Douglass explained it: "They thought it a violation of anti-slavery principles, conceding the right of property in man, and a wasteful expenditure of money." Poignantly, Douglass goes on at length to defend his acceptance of the payment for his freedom, morally and economically (Douglass, 1881, pp. 259–60).

31 Douglass, 1881, pp. 261–68. There was much resistance among the New England abolitionists (including Garrison and Phillips) to his setting up a newspaper: they felt it was not needed, bound to fail, and that Douglass was better suited as a speaker than a writer. Some thought his "persistence an unwarrantable ambition and presumption." But he persevered, mostly with English support. His printing establishment cost nearly $1,000 to set up.

To keep peace, he moved the newspaper to Rochester, New York, so its local circulation would not interfere with the already popular *Liberator* and *Anti-Slavery Standard*. *The North Star* weekly was founded in autumn 1847, and had an average circulation of 3,000. According to Quarles (Douglass, 1845, p. ix), it was the first black-owned newspaper in America.

Douglass continued to be assisted by friends abroad and at home. After the first three and a half years, the paper's name was changed to *Frederick Douglass' Paper*, to distinguish it from the many other abolitionist papers with similar titles. It existed for almost sixteen years, "till the union of the States was assured and emancipation was a fact accomplished" (Douglass, 1881, pp. 261–68).

The caption for panel 21 alludes to Martin Van Buren, eighth president of the United States and candidate of the Free Soil party, with its goals of "free soil, free speech, free labor, and free men." The party was organized in Buffalo in 1848, and the Free Soil Convention was held in Pittsburgh in 1852; Douglass was a speaker and "drew the loudest applause" (Quarles, *Black Abolitionists*, pp. 185–86).

The Fugitive Slave Law is discussed in note 3 above.

Dred Scott, a Missouri slave, sued the government for his freedom after being taken into free territory. Chief Justice Taney of the Supreme Court delivered the Dred Scott Decision in March 1857, throwing out Scott's case on grounds that a slave could not be a citizen of the United States and thus had no standing in federal court. He further restated that slaves were recognized as property by the Constitution, and one of the constitutional functions of Congress was the protection of property in the territories. At an American Anti-Slavery Society annual meeting in New York, May 1857, Douglass characterized the Dred Scott Decision as a "judicial incarnation of wolfishness," the product of the "slave-holding wing of the Supreme Court" (Quarles, *Black Abolitionists*, pp. 230–34).

The original 1938–39 caption to panel 21, which has been published several times in the literature (as "panel 22"), mistakenly was worded to say that *The North Star* was "the first Negro paper." In fact, many black newspapers were published before the Civil War, beginning in about the 1820s. According to Quarles (*Black Abolitionists*, pp. 84–89), the first two black weeklies were the *Freedom's Journal* and *The Rights of All*. Freedom and equality were the common themes. Usually these papers were short-lived because of financial problems. *The North Star* received the most financial support, but it was forced to terminate in 1860. Others included *The Colored American*, *The Mirrors of Liberty*, and *The Provincial Freeman*.

32 Douglass, 1881, pp. 271–72. According to historian Philip Foner, Douglass made some of his most important contributions to the antislavery cause in his capacity of superintendent of the Underground Railroad in Rochester, the hub of a network of routes northward to Canada. In 1847 when Douglass returned from England and settled in Rochester, his house became an extremely important station, and by 1850 he was leader of the network in Rochester (Foner, *Frederick Douglass*, pp. 129 ff.).

33 Douglass, 1881, p. 272.

34 Douglass, 1881, p. 278. According to Foner, *Frederick Douglass*, pp. 137–38, Douglass first met John Brown while on a lecture tour in New England. Brown was a merchant in Springfield, Massachusetts. He was aware of Douglass's work and sought his cooperation in his plan to achieve the abolishment of slavery through a guerrilla network in the mountains. Douglass (in Douglass, 1881, pp. 278–79) was struck by Brown's physical appearance and impressed by his fervor. Before their meeting in 1847, Douglass had maintained that slavery could be abolished peacefully, but afterward, as seeds of doubt grew, in his speeches Douglass began to speak of destroying slavery through bloodshed, a viewpoint representing a disagreement with some of his abolitionist friends, including Sojourner Truth. Douglass and Brown met many times over the years and were friends.

35 Hugh Forbes, *New York Herald*, October 29, 1859, quoted in Jules Abels, *Man on Fire: John Brown and the Cause of Liberty*, New York, p. i.

36 Three weeks before the Harper's Ferry raid (October 16, 1859), John Brown met with Douglass in a stone quarry near Chambersburg, Pennsylvania, to officially present the plan to him. Douglass did not join Brown, believing that Brown "was about to rivet the fetters more firmly on the limbs of the enslaved." Douglass, 1881, pp. 320–30, spends many pages explaining his relationship with Brown, his admiration for him, his reasons for not being a member of the Harper's Ferry raid, and his reasons for going to England.

37 Although Douglass respected Abraham Lincoln highly, in his autobiography (1881, pp. 330–38) he clearly states his grievances against Lincoln's indecisive program and approach to maintaining the Union. In fact, Douglass's views on many historical figures, among them Daniel Webster and Andrew Johnson, are most enlightening (see Douglass, 1892, index).

38 Through his newspaper, Frederick Douglass encouraged Northern blacks to join the Union forces. For example, the words used in the caption for panel 26 were part of a speech he reprinted in the March 2, 1863, issue of *Douglass' Monthly*, successor to *The North Star* and *Frederick Douglass' Paper* (see Douglass, 1881, pp. 344–46, for the reprinted speech). Douglass's two sons Charles and Lewis were the first to enlist in New York State in the 54th Regiment, and a third son Frederick recruited troops in the Mississippi valley (Douglass, 1881, pp. 347 and 355).

Lawrence's caption for panel 26 alludes to Shields Green and John Anthony Copeland, Jr., two black participants in the Harper's Ferry raid who were captured and hung along with Brown (Quarles, *Allies for Freedom: Blacks and*

John Brown, pp. 96–97). Denmark Vesey and Nat Turner were leaders and martyrs in slave uprisings, and were legendary inspirations for all enslaved blacks (Quarles, *Allies*, p. 64).

39 Douglass, 1881, pp. 347 ff.; Quarles, *Frederick Douglass*, pp. 210–11.

The image in panel 27 had always been a mystery to me: what is it? Even the artist couldn't recall. After quite a bit of sleuthing, I found a photograph of a nineteenth century sculpture, taken from a different angle, in an American art history text. The sculpture *Freedom* was created by American artist Thomas Crawford and was mounted on the Capitol dome in 1863. It is 19 feet high and is made of cast bronze. For a discussion of the piece, see Oliver W. Larkin, *Art and Life in America* (New York: Rinehart & Company, 1949), p. 184.

Although 1863 is the year that Douglass met with Lincoln and he may have witnessed the mounting of the sculpture on the Capitol dome, I could find no mention of this in Douglass's writings.

40 Douglass makes the point that in the North, the war was fought for the first two years as a pro-slavery battle of conciliation and that the Proclamation of Emancipation (January 1, 1863) established that all compromises with slavery must end. It was this abrupt change that led to violence and bloody riots in the North (Douglass, 1881, pp. 356–62).

Historian John Hope Franklin has made the point to me that the New York riots were caused by fear among whites that they would be drafted to fight in a war that would free the slaves who would then compete with them for jobs. The riots are also known as the New York draft riots; personal communication, September 5, 1990.

41 When the war ended, Douglass worked to obtain citizenship and the right to vote for blacks (Douglass, 1881, pp. 384 ff.). The Fourteenth Amendment (July 28, 1868) gave blacks citizenship, and the Fifteenth Amendment (March 30, 1870) gave black males the right to vote.

42 The wording of the first part of panel 30's caption is derived from Douglass, 1881, pp. 427 ff. According to Douglass, the opposition to his appointment to this office was based on race and took many forms: there were efforts in the Senate to block his appointment, the press harassed him, he received personal slights, and there was a petition to President Hayes for his removal.

43 Douglass, 1881, p. 436; Douglass explains his attitude toward the exodus on pp. 435 ff. Douglass spoke out against the reasons for the exodus at the Social Science Congress at Saratoga, New York, on September 12, 1879. See Foner, *Life and Writings of Frederick Douglass*, Volume IV, pp. 105–13, for a discussion of the exodus and pp. 324–42 for a reproduction of Douglass's speech. The speech is also reproduced in part in Douglass, 1881, pp. 437–44. The quote in caption 31 is loosely adapted from the speech, pp. 441–42.

44 Douglass, 1881, p. 448.

45 Foner, *Life and Writings*, Vol. I, pp. 12–13.

46 Quarles, 1960, in Douglass, 1845, p. xvii.

3

The *Harriet Tubman* Series (1939–40) (pp. 31–41)

Notes for the *Frederick Douglass* and *Harriet Tubman* series include explanations of issues and persons alluded to in the captions to the paintings, as well as further interpretations of the paintings' content.

Valuable sources for biographical information on Harriet Tubman were Sarah Bradford, *Harriet Tubman: The Moses of Her People* (Secaucus, New Jersey: Citadel Press, 1961 [1886]), and Earl Conrad's two biographies, *Harriet Tubman: Negro Soldier and Abolitionist* (New York: International Publishers Inc., 1942) and *Harriet Tubman* (New York: The Associated Publishers, 1943). The 1943 Conrad account is the most definitive of those available. Bradford's book first appeared in 1869 in a short form (*Scenes in the Life of Harriet Tubman*), and it was then expanded in 1886; both versions were privately printed by Bradford to raise funds for Harriet Tubman.

The epigraph for this chapter comes from statements made by Jacob Lawrence in conversation with the author, April 17, 1988.

1 As in the case of Frederick Douglass, there is uncertainty about Harriet Tubman's birth date. According to Conrad, 1942, p. 5, she was born about 1820. Butler A. Jones, in his introduction to Bradford, 1961, p. viii, says that she was born in 1820 or 1821. Bucktown, Maryland, was her home town; see Conrad, 1942, p. 21.

2 See above, note 3 to Chapter 2, "The *Frederick Douglass* Series," for a discussion of the Fugitive Slave Law.

3 Aaron Douglas is discussed in Wheat, *Jacob Lawrence, American Painter*, 1986; see index, s.v.

4 The Reverend Henry Ward Beecher was a renowned anti-slavery worker and moral crusader beginning in the 1840s. A preacher at Plymouth Church, Brooklyn, he wrote a widely read book on temperance and was known for his stirring oratory. See Filler, *Crusade*, pp. 155, 195–96, 241.

5 Henry Clay became secretary of state in 1824. Early on, in the late 1790s, he worked to end slavery in Kentucky, but by the late 1830s he was interested in appeasing the South. This quote comes from a speech Clay gave in the U.S. Senate on February 7, 1839, on the subject of abolition petitions, in which he summed up the pro-slavery argument against gradual or immediate emancipation. See Filler, *Crusade*, pp. 12, 20, 82, 150.

6 The invention of the cotton gin in 1793 by Eli Whitney had a profound influence on the institution of slavery in the United States. Without that development, slavery might have come to an end much sooner. As a result of the cotton gin, the Southern planters enlarged their plantations, put more laborers to work in the fields, and raised more cotton to send to textile mills: slaves were even more exploited and slavery more entrenched than before.

Tobacco, not cotton, was the main crop grown in Maryland, both Douglass's and Tubman's home ground. Here, Lawrence uses cotton as a broad symbol of the South and of slavery.

7 The artist is often asked which figure is Harriet in panel 4; he says it does not matter. The caption for panel 4 is a free adaptation of Sarah Bradford's words, 1961, p. 13. According to Professor S. M. Hopkins, Auburn Theological Seminary (and Bradford's brother), Harriet Tubman was of pure African descent, of a tribe on the Guinea coast, perhaps the Fellatas (Bradford, 1961, and Preface, 1886, p. 9). Conrad, 1969, p. 3, says Harriet Tubman was probably of Ashanti or Fellata background.

8 Conrad, 1943, discusses Harriet Tubman's appearance and dress on pp. 11–12, 21, 22.

9 Lawrence does not recall whether he was inspired by the 1860s illustration. On the title page of Conrad, 1942, a note says that the woodcut rendition of Harriet Tubman derives from a photo of her taken in 1863. A search of archival collections (e.g., the Schomburg Collection) does not reveal this photo.

10 Filler, *Crusade*, n.p. See above, note 38, for "The *Frederick Douglass* Series," for a discussion of Nat Turner.

11 Conrad, 1943, pp. 24, 35.

12 Conrad, 1943, pp. 35–38, and Bradford, 1961, pp. 29–30, discuss Harriet's escape. Harriet Tubman's age at the time of her escape (like the date of her birth) is problematic. Bradford, 1961, says she was between twenty and twenty-five (p. 26). Conrad, 1943, says (regarding the reward notice date) that she would have been about twenty-nine.

13 Lawrence, in conversation with the author, April 17, 1988.

14 The caption for panel 13 is adapted from Bradford, 1961, pp. 30–32.

15 Brief allusion to a woman helping Harriet Tubman can be found in Conrad, 1942, p. 9. Not much is clear about this woman. Conrad, 1943, p. 37, mentions a white woman from whom Harriet initially received some aid and who helped her get away, but this was at the beginning of her journey, not after she reached the North, as is implied in Lawrence's captions here. The "strange room, round and tapering to a peak" mentioned in the caption for panel 14, according to my research, may very well allude to the top floor of a Shaker circular stone barn. Some of these structures in the early nineteenth century were topped by a hexagonal wooden cupola with a pronounced twelve-sided interior wooden superstructure. One still exists in Hancock, Massachusetts, dating from 1826, and is illustrated in Daniel Mendelowitz, *A History of American Art* (New York: Holt, Rinehart & Winston, Inc., 1970), p. 157.

16 On seeing this painting for the first time in almost twenty years, Gwendolyn Knight Lawrence remarked that it was a very "elegant" work and Jacob agreed. The Lawrences, in conversation with the author, April 17, 1988.

17 Conrad, 1943, pp. 40–41.

18 Bradford, 1961, pp. 111–12.

19 Still's secret records of the fugitives who passed through Philadelphia are among the only historical records of the names, dates, origins, and destinations of those in flight. William Still published a chronicle of slave narratives around 1860 called *The Underground Railroad*. For mention of William Still, see Conrad, 1942, pp. 15–16; Conrad, 1943, pp. 40–41, 102; Quarles, *Black Abolitionists*, p. 59; and Ripley, *Black Abolitionist Papers* volumes (see index).

20 Black conductors are discussed by Conrad, 1943, pp. 25 ff. Bradford, 1961, p. 33, refers to Harriet's use of a gun to urge on the fugitives.

21 Conrad, 1942, p. 14.

22 Conrad, 1942, p. 26.

23 Conrad referred to the writer of the letter, Colonel Thomas Wentworth Higginson, as "the best historian of the abolition." He was an active abolitionist who later led black troops in the Civil War. See Conrad, 1943, pp. 26, 70.

24 See above, note 4, "The *Frederick Douglass* Series," for a

discussion of the English abolition movement and the Emancipation Bill of 1833 See also note 3 above, "The *Frederick Douglass* Series," for a discussion of the Fugitive Slave Law.

25 Conrad, 1943, pp. 45–49. The image for this painting was probably inspired by Harriet's story about a particularly cold trip during which she and her charges waded many icy streams; Harriet had to travel long distances in wet clothing and afterward was very ill for a long period of time (Bradford, 1961, pp. 74–75; Conrad, 1942, pp. 19–20). A well-known article on Tubman published in the *Boston Commonwealth* in 1862 also refers to "the snows of the Canadian forest" (see Bradford, 1961, p. 112). The editor of that periodical was Franklin B. Sanborn, who also wrote a biography of John Brown; he knew Harriet Tubman personally. His article was one of the usual sources of information on Harriet Tubman's life, and Lawrence would have read it in the Schomburg Collection.

26 The first quote in this paragraph comes from Conrad, 1943, p. 108. The second quote comes from the notes of James Yerrington, secretary of the Massachusetts Anti-Slavery Society, in Conrad, 1943, pp. 109–11. According to Conrad, 1943, p. 101, records starting in 1858 reveal that Harriet Tubman first addressed small gatherings of abolitionist sympathizers in central New York. Tubman spoke before a women's suffrage convention in 1860. The second sentence of caption 21 is adapted from Robert W. Taylor, *Harriet Tubman, The Heroine in Ebony* (n.d.), quoted in Conrad, 1943, p. 146.

27 The information on Thomas Garrett comes from Filler, *Crusade*, pp. 123, 163. Bradford, 1961, pp. 39 ff., discusses at length a fugitive named Joe because he impressed Harriet Tubman so much; he was enormously tall and strong and is probably the person seated at the table on the left in Garrett's house, panel 22.

28 Bradford, 1961, pp. 44–45.

29 Bradford, 1961, pp. 44–50.

30 Conrad, 1942, discusses Tubman's parents' escape (p. 91) and her speaking career (p. 25); see also Conrad, 1943, pp. 109–11.

31 According to Conrad, 1943, p. 71, Harriet Tubman arrived in Boston first in 1854; Conrad takes his facts in this instance from the contemporaneous nineteenth century black historian William Wells Brown. She again traveled throughout New England in 1859 to speak against slavery (Conrad, 1943, pp. 106–109). Such historical facts are reported inconsistently in the literature and are therefore difficult to establish for Tubman.

32 Conrad, 1942, p. 28, discusses "General Tubman." There are conflicting opinions about when and how Harriet Tubman met John Brown. According to Conrad, 1943, p. 115, Frederick Douglass met with John Brown in Rochester and Douglass urged him to meet Harriet. It was arranged that the Reverend Loguen would accompany John Brown to St. Catharines, Ontario, Canada. The meeting took place there on about April 4 or 5, 1858. According to Quarles (*Black Abolitionists*, p. 59, and *Frederick Douglass*, p. 239), Harriet Tubman and John Brown met at the Chatham Convention in Ontario in May 1858. Other accounts lead one to believe that Douglass came with John Brown to Canada. John Brown's letter to his son, in which he discusses the meeting, says he was with Loguen (see Conrad, 1943, p. 115). The caption to panel 25 implies that Frederick Douglass is the person on the right in the painting, but it could be the Reverend Loguen.

Bradford, 1961, alludes briefly to Harriet Tubman's relationship with John Brown on p. 96. According to Franklin B. Sanborn, *Boston Commonwealth*, 1862, Harriet Tubman and John Brown also met in Boston, in the winter of 1858–59, where she aided him in obtaining recruits among her people, and money. She agreed to get more recruits and meet with him in two weeks, and they kept in touch through Frederick Douglass (see Bradford, 1961, p. 117).

33 Conrad, 1942, p. 34; 1943, pp. 149–53.

34 Conrad, 1942, p. 37; 1943, pp. 158–64. According to Conrad, the newly freed slaves became jealous of Tubman's privileges to draw rations as a soldier. She gave up those privileges to eliminate this problem.

35 Conrad, 1943, pp. 160–64; 1942, 37 and 39; Bradford, 1961, p. 102.

36 Bradford, 1961, p. 98; Conrad, 1942, p. 37.

37 The Bradford biography is discussed in Bradford, 1961, p. 95; Conrad, 1943, p. 182. Tubman's life after the war is discussed in Conrad, 1942, pp. 43 ff., and 1943, pp. 185 ff. Tubman's second husband is mentioned in Conrad, 1943, pp. 181, 206–07.

38 Conrad, 1943, discusses Frederick Douglass's death and the women's movement, pp. 213–14, and Tubman's death, pp. 224–26.

39 Bradford, 1961, 134–35, publishes the letter by Frederick Douglass, along with others from Gerrit Smith, Wendell Phillips, Franklin B. Sanborn, William H. Seward, and other persons, in an appendix. The letters were offered by Bradford as corroboration for Harriet Tubman's account of the incidents in her life and testimony to her character "for the satisfaction of the incredulous" (pp. 4–5).

40 For example, see Conrad, 1943, p. 70.

41 Panels with touches of humor and/or light-hearted imagery deftly spaced between paintings with disturbing presentations are, e.g., panels 4, 8, 13, 19, 21., 22 (the shoes), and 28.

42 Bradford, 1961, p. 4.

43 Douglass, 1881, pp. 476–77.

44 Conrad, 1943, pp. 111–12; the entire passage makes these points even more forcefully.

45 Lawrence, lecture, November 15, 1982.

46 There are also many differences between the two series. Primarily, because the later illustrations were for children, the artist modifies his approach: he includes more humorous touches and many animals. Also, after his African trips in 1962–64, Lawrence's art exhibits exaggerated anatomy of figures, crablike hands, and strenuously articulated feet.

47 Quoted in Barbara Seese, "The Black Experience—Pictures Tell the Story," University of Washington *Daily* (October 1978).

48 These works (about four or five) are drawings and paintings of special impact. See Wheat, *Jacob Lawrence, American Painter*, index, for more discussion of the use of the Harriet Tubman theme in Lawrence's work.

49 Lawrence's *Self-Portrait* (1977) is reproduced in Wheat, *Jacob Lawrence, American Painter*, p. 175.

50 Lawrence in conversation with the author, April 17, 1988.

4

The Imagery of Struggle (pp. 43–46)

The epigraph for this chapter is taken from Elizabeth McCausland, "Jacob Lawrence," *Magazine of Art*, 38, November 1945, p. 254.

1 The *Toussaint L'Ouverture* series (1937–38) and the *John Brown* series (1941) are similar in some of these qualities.

2 Forceful didactic content in Lawrence's work also appeared in the late 1940s, when he did several drawings on racism, in the 1960s when he did many works on the Civil Rights struggle in America, and in the *Hiroshima* series of 1983, a statement of protest against nuclear warfare.

3 For a discussion of Giotto's use of wit, which is very similar to Lawrence's, see Andrew Landis, "The Legend of Giotto's Wit and the Arena Chapel," *Art Bulletin* 68, December 1986, pp. 581–96.

4 Jane Van Cleve, "The Human Views of Jacob Lawrence," *Stepping Out Northwest*, Winter 1982, pp. 36–37.

5 Lawrence in conversation with the author, April 17, 1988, and lecture, Hirshhorn Museum and Sculpture Garden, April 18, 1988.

6 Jacob Lawrence, "The Artist Responds," *The Crisis*, August-September 1970, pp. 266–67.

Chronology

1917   Born Atlantic City, New Jersey.

1919   Moved to Pennsylvania.

1930   Moved to New York City's Harlem.

1932–37   Studied at WPA-sponsored Harlem Art Workshops.

1936   Painted first significant works, Harlem scenes.

1937–39   Studied at American Artists School, New York. Painted first series, *Toussaint L'Ouverture*.

1938–39   Worked as easel painter on WPA Federal Art Project.

1941   Married Gwendolyn Knight, painter and sculptor. Traveled to the South. Joined Downtown Gallery, New York.

1943–45   World War II, served in U.S. Coast Guard as combat artist; traveled on troop ship to Europe, Near East, India.

1944   First major one-person exhibition, Museum of Modern Art, New York.

1946   Received Guggenheim Fellowship to paint *War* series. Taught at Black Mountain College, North Carolina, the beginning of his teaching career.

1954–70   Taught at Skowhegan School of Painting and Sculpture, Maine; Pratt Institute, New York; Five Towns Music and Art Foundation, Long Island; Brandeis University, Waltham, Massachusetts; New School for Social Research, New York; Art Students League, New York; California State University, Hayward; University of Washington, Seattle.

1960   First retrospective exhibition, Brooklyn Museum, New York (toured nationally).

1964   Lived and worked in Nigeria.

1971   Appointed full professor, School of Art, University of Washington; moved to Seattle, where he still lives and works.

1974   Traveling retrospective, Whitney Museum of American Art, New York.

1978   Appointed commissioner, National Council of the Arts (six-year term).

1979   Created first mural, *Games*, Kingdome Stadium, Seattle, Washington.

1983   Elected member, American Academy of Arts and Letters.

1986   Traveling retrospective, Seattle Art Museum.

1987   Retired from teaching. Professor Emeritus, School of Art, University of Washington.

1989   Seventh mural installed, *Community*, Government Services Administration building, Jamaica, New York.

1990   Completed his fifteenth series, *Eight Sermons of the Creation from the Book of Genesis*. Received National Medal of Arts from President George Bush.

Selected Bibliography

JACOB LAWRENCE

Archives of American Art, Jacob Lawrence Material, Smithsonian Institution, Washington, D.C.

Bearden, Romare, and Harry Henderson. *Six Black Masters of American Art*. Garden City, New York: Doubleday and Co., 1972.

Berman, Avis. "Jacob Lawrence and the Making of Americans." *Artnews* 83 (February 1984): 78–86.

Brown, Milton W. *Jacob Lawrence* (exhibition catalog). New York: Whitney Museum of American Art, 1974.

Driskell, David. *Two Centuries of Black American Art* (exhibition catalog). New York: Alfred A. Knopf, 1976.

Fax, Elton C. *Seventeen Black Artists*. New York: Dodd, Mead and Co., 1971.

Fine, Elsa Honig. *The Afro-American Artist*. New York: Holt, Rinehart and Winston, 1973.

Fisk, Carol (producer), and Ray Carlton (director). *Jacob Lawrence: American Artist* (videotape). Atlanta: Georgia Public Television, 1986.

Greene, Carroll, Jr. "Interview with Jacob Lawrence." Washington, D.C.: Archives of American Art, Smithsonian Institution, October 25, 1968.

"Jacob Lawrence." *Ebony* 6 (April 1951): 73–78.

Kramer, Hilton. "Art: Lawrence Epics of Blacks." *The New York Times* (June 1974).

———. "Chronicles of Black History." *The New York Times* (May 26, 1974): 17.

Larkin, Oliver. *Art and Life in America*. 2d ed. New York: Holt, Rinehart and Winston, 1960.

Lawrence, Jacob. *Harriet and the Promised Land*. New York: Windmill Books/Simon and Schuster, 1968.

———. Lecture to students (tape), University of Washington, Seattle, November 15, 1982 (Ellen Wheat, Jacob Lawrence archival materials).

Lewis, Samella. *Art: African American*. New York: Harcourt Brace Jovanovich, 1978.

———. *Jacob Lawrence* (exhibition catalog). Santa Monica, California: The Museum of African American Art, 1982.

Lewis, Samella, and Lester Sullivan. *Black Art* 5:3 (1982), issue devoted to Jacob Lawrence.

Louchheim, Aline B. "Lawrence: Quiet Spokesman." *Art News* 43 (October 15, 1944): 14.

———. "An Artist Reports on the Troubled Mind." *The New York Times Magazine* (October 15, 1950): 15, 16, 36, 38.

———. (Saarinen, Aline L.). *Jacob Lawrence* (retrospective exhibition catalog). New York: American Federation of Arts, 1960.

McCausland, Elizabeth. "Jacob Lawrence." *Magazine of Art* 38 (November 1945): 250–54.

Saarinen, Aline L. (see *Louchheim*, 1960).

Wheat, Ellen Harkins. "Jacob Lawrence, American Painter." Master's Thesis, University of Washington, Seattle, May 1983.

———. "Jacob Lawrence." Ph.D. Dissertation, University of Washington, Seattle, June 1986.

———. *Jacob Lawrence, American Painter*. Seattle: University of Washington Press, 1986. This monograph was published simultaneously with the opening of the retrospective exhibition "Jacob Lawrence, American Painter" initiated by the author for the Seattle Art Museum.

FREDERICK DOUGLASS

Baker, Houston, editor, *The Narrative and Selected Writings of Frederick Douglass*. New York: Penguin, 1982.

Blassingame, John W. *The Frederick Douglass Papers*, Vol. I. New Haven, Connecticut: Yale University Press, 1985.

Bontemps, Arna. *Free at Last: The Life of Frederick Douglass*. New York: Dodd, Mead & Company, 1971.

Davidson, Margaret. *Frederick Douglass Fights for Freedom*. New York: Scholastic Inc., 1968 (for young readers).

Douglass, Frederick. *Narrative of the Life of Frederick Douglass, An American Slave, Written by Himself* (1845). Benjamin Quarles, editor. Cambridge, Mass.: Harvard University Press, 1960.

——. *My Bondage and My Freedom* (1855). New York: Arno Press, 1968. Portrait, illustrated.

——. *Life and Times of Frederick Douglass, Written by Himself* (1881). Facsimile edition with introduction by George L. Ruffin, 1881. Secaucus, N.J.: Citadel Press, 1983. Portrait, illustrated.

——. *Life and Times of Frederick Douglass, Written by Himself* (1892 Revised Edition). Introduction by Rayford W. Logan, 1962. New York: MacMillan Publishing Company, 1962. Portrait, index.

Foner, Philip S. *The Life and Writings of Frederick Douglass,* Vols. I–V. New York: International Publishers, 1950–75. Portrait, bibliography, chronology.

——. *Frederick Douglass: A Biography,* 1950. New York: The Citadel Press, 1969.

Huggins, Nathan Irvin. *Slave and Citizen: The Life of Frederick Douglass.* Boston: Little, Brown and Company, 1980. Comprehensive annotated bibliography, index.

Preston, Dickson J. *Young Frederick Douglass: The Maryland Years.* Baltimore: The Johns Hopkins University Press, 1980. Portrait, chronology, comprehensive notes and bibliography, index.

Quarles, Benjamin. *Frederick Douglass,* 1948. Preface by James M. McPherson, 1968. New York: Atheneum, 1970. Portrait, bibliography, and index.

Russell, Sharman Apt. *Frederick Douglass.* New York: Chelsea House, 1988 (for young readers).

Harriet Tubman

Bradford, Sarah H. *Scenes in the Life of Harriet Tubman.* Auburn, New York: W. J. Moses, Printer, 1869. Portrait.

——. *Harriet Tubman: The Moses of Her People,* 1886. Introduction by Butler A. Jones, 1961. Secaucus, N.J.: The Citadel Press, 1961. Portrait.

Conrad, Earl. *Harriet Tubman: Negro Soldier and Abolitionist.* New York: International Publishers, 1942. Portrait.

——. *Harriet Tubman.* Washington, D.C.: The Associated Publishers, 1943. Bibliographic notes.

Ferris, Jeri. *Go Free or Die: A Story About Harriet Tubman.* Minneapolis: Carolrhoda Books, 1988 (for young readers).

Krane, Susan. *Jacob Lawrence: The Harriet Tubman Series* (exhibition catalog). Buffalo, New York: Albright-Knox Art Gallery, 1986. Bibliographic notes.

Lawrence, Jacob. *Harriet and the Promised Land.* New York: Windmill Books/Simon and Schuster, Inc., 1968.

Smith, Kathie Billingslea. *Harriet Tubman.* New York: Little Simon/Simon & Schuster, 1988 (for young readers).

Related History

Abels, Jules. *Man on Fire: John Brown and the Cause of Liberty.* New York: The Macmillan Company, 1917.

Blockson, Charles L. "Escape from Slavery: The Underground Railroad." *National Geographic,* 166:1 (July 1984): 38 ff.

Filler, Louis. *The Crusade Against Slavery: 1830–1860.* New York: Harper & Brothers, 1960.

Levine, Ellen. *. . . If You Traveled on the Underground Railroad.* New York: Scholastic Inc., 1988 (for young readers).

Oates, Stephen B. *To Purge This Land with Blood: A Biography of John Brown.* New York: Harper & Row, 1970.

Pease, Jane H., and William H. Pease. *The Fugitive Slave Law and Anthony Burns: A Problem in Law Enforcement.* New York: J. B. Lippincott Company, 1975.

Quarles, Benjamin. *Black Abolitionists.* New York: Oxford University Press, 1969.

——. *Allies for Freedom: Blacks and John Brown.* New York: Oxford University Press, 1974.

Ripley, C. Peter, editor. *The Black Abolitionist Papers*, Vol. II: Canada, 1830–1865. Chapel Hill: The University of North Carolina Press, 1986.

Sanborn, Franklin B., editor. *The Life and Letters of John Brown, Liberator of Kansas and Martyr of Virginia*. Boston: Roberts Brothers, 1885.

Siebert, Wilbur H. *The Underground Railroad from Slavery to Freedom*. Gloucester, Mass.: P. Smith, 1898.

Smedley, R. C. *History of the Underground Railroad*, 1883. Introduction by William Loren Katz, 1969. New York: Arno Press, 1969. This work is of limited value because it confines its interest to white abolitionists.

Still, William. *The Underground Railroad*. Philadelphia: Porter & Coates, 1872.

Index

This book has been published on the occasion of the traveling exhibition, "Jacob Lawrence: The *Frederick Douglass* and *Harriet Tubman* Series of 1938–40," 1991–93. At the time of publication, venues for the show included:

Memorial Art Gallery of the University of Rochester
Rochester, New York
(February 16 – April 14, 1991)

Philadelphia Museum of Art
Philadelphia, Pennsylvania
(May 4 – June 30, 1991)

The Studio Museum of Harlem
New York, New York
(August 1 – November 5, 1991)

The Baltimore Museum of Art
Baltimore, Maryland
(November 26, 1991 – February 23, 1992)

Delaware Art Museum
Wilmington, Delaware
(March 6 – April 2, 1991)

The Art Institute of Chicago
Chicago, Illinois
(May 13 – August 2, 1992)

The Carnegie Museum of Art
Pittsburgh, Pennsylvania
(early 1993)

LIBRARY OF CONGRESS CATALOGING-IN-PUBLICATION DATA

Wheat, Ellen Harkins.
    Jacob Lawrence: the Frederick Douglass and Harriet Tubman series
of 1938–40 / Ellen Harkins Wheat.
        p.   cm.
    Includes bibliographical references.
    ISBN 0-9616982-4-1
    ISBN 0-9816982-5-x (pbk.)
    1. Lawrence, Jacob, 1917–   —Criticism and interpretation.
2. Douglass, Frederick, 1817?–1895—Portraits.   3. Tubman, Harriet,
1820?–1913—Portraits.   4. Afro-Americans—Portraits.   I. Title.
ND237.L29W48   1991
759.13—dc20
                                                    90–23494
                                                     CIP